THAT'S MY TEAM!

THAT'S MY TEAM!

THE HISTORY, SCIENCE, AND FUN BEHIND SPORTS TEAMS' NAMES

Paul Volponi

ROWMAN & LITTLEFIELD
Lanham • Boulder • New York • London

Published by Rowman & Littlefield
An imprint of The Rowman & Littlefield Publishing Group, Inc.
4501 Forbes Boulevard, Suite 200, Lanham, Maryland 20706
www.rowman.com

6 Tinworth Street, London, SE11 5AL, United Kingdom

British Library Cataloguing in Publication Information Available

Library of Congress Cataloging-in-Publication Data

Names: Volponi, Paul, author.
Title: That's my team! : the history, science, and fun behind sports teams' names / Paul Volponi.
Description: Lanham, Maryland : Rowman & Littlefield, [2019] | Includes bibliographical references and index.
Identifiers: LCCN 2019000246 (print) | LCCN 2019017640 (ebook) | ISBN 9781538126745 (Electronic) | ISBN 9781538126738 (cloth : alk. paper)
Subjects: LCSH: Sports teams—United States—History. | Sports teams—United States—Names—History.
Classification: LCC GV583 (ebook) | LCC GV583 .V65 2019 (print) | DDC 796.06—dc23
LC record available at https://lccn.loc.gov/2019000246

∞™ The paper used in this publication meets the minimum requirements of American National Standard for Information Sciences—Permanence of Paper for Printed Library Materials, ANSI/NISO Z39.48-1992.

Printed in the United States of America

Thank you to the people throughout my life who encouraged me to write:

Paul Volponi Sr.
Mary Volponi
April Volponi
Sabrina Volponi
Adam Weiss
Angelo Spanodemos
Andrea Orsini
Rosemary Stimola
Lenny Shulman
Evan Hammonds
Christen Karniski

CONTENTS

CONTENTS

AUTHOR'S NOTE

I grew up pretending to read the books my teachers gave me—all through middle school and high school. I was a really good reader, but the assigned books didn't motivate me. So I listened to the discussion about the books in class in order to get a passing grade. That sharpened my skills as a listener. As a result, I became fascinated by language and the idea of story. I took that love of language to the basketball court. As a street basketball player in New York City, my ears soaked up the sounds of spoken stories. I knew the nickname of every pro and college team, not only in basketball but in all sports. When I became an English teacher, I took those team names and their origins into the classroom to share with my students. This book was born of that collective journey. I hope we can walk together through these pages, and that you will allow me to be your personal guide to those magical moments when sports meets knowledge.

INTRODUCTION

Who's in a name? Plenty. There's pride, passion, and a sense of identity. Perhaps there is no greater association with names in our society than in the arena of sports. Yet individual players' names sewn onto the back of uniforms ultimately fade behind the team names emblazoned across the front. Even legendary sports heroes such as Michael Jordan, Jackie Robinson, Tom Brady, and soccer's Mia Hamm take their place beneath the banners of Chicago Bulls, Brooklyn Dodgers, New England Patriots, and Team USA.

Sports fans are rarely shy about proclaiming their loyalties. T-shirts, jerseys, jackets, and caps provide open testimony for all to see. For many fans, the pronoun *we* has replaced *they*: "We won!" "We lost!" "We're #1!" It's a true tribute to the unifying nature of sports. And at the heart of every such connection is a team name. Such affiliations can forge lifelong bonds, extending from the playing fields and stands into the streets and collective consciousness of the surrounding city. The chasm separating Cubs fans on the North Side of Chicago from White Sox fans on the South Side can run as deep and wide as any natural divide.

Rivalries and factions based on team names inserted after the word "Go!" can literally fracture households. But when the pull is strong enough, even the allegiance of boundaries can be overcome. Yes, the visitors can actually garner cheers over the home team. And as the overwhelmingly popular Dallas Cowboys championship squads of the 1990s can attest, it is indeed possible to become America's Team.

If you take the time to examine the nicknames of your favorite professional and college sports teams, you'll discover that they've been inspired by history, science, literature, music, and a slew of other subjects. That's right. The teams for which you root read like an encyclopedia of learning.

Nicknames can be created in any number of fashions. Baseball's Colorado Rockies recognize an outstanding geological feature—the Rocky Mountains. Football's Pittsburgh Steelers are an example of a name inspired by a regional occupation—Pennsylvania's steel industry. Some teams, such as the Boston Celtics and Sad Diego State Aztecs, are named after people who influenced a particular city or region. Today, however, the debate rages over the appropriateness of teams named after Native American culture. Nicknames such as Indians, Braves, and, of course, Redskins, remain at the center of the controversy.

Franchises that have moved from one city to another aren't obligated to change their nicknames. That can create some head-scratching combinations, such as the puzzling Utah Jazz of professional basketball. (Jazz has its roots in Utah? *Really?*)

What historical events are behind names such as the Philadelphia 76ers, San Francisco 49ers, and Oklahoma Sooners? How do the names of women's professional teams today differ from those of the 1940s? What inspired the owner of the Washington Bullets to change his team's name to the Wizards? How did the University of Florida's nickname impact the sports drink Gatorade?

Together, we will answer these questions and many more as we explore the significance of the names bestowed upon our favorite sports teams. Along the way we will encounter a number of challenges that will exercise our minds and our creativity. We'll even have several opportunities at a rather unique challenge—giving a brand-new sports franchise a fitting and inspiring name. But most of all, we will celebrate the moving, thought-provoking, and powerful nature of these nicknames that make you leap to your feet and shout, "That's my team!"

1

WORLD HISTORY

WARRING PARTIES

The origins of football, or *futballe*, can be traced back to the beginning of the second century in England. After an occupation of more than twenty years, English forces finally drove out the invading Danes. Years later, Danish skulls, unearthed from English battlefields, were kicked about the countryside for sport. Eventually the skulls were replaced with inflated cow bladders. Contests emerged between neighboring towns. The object was to kick these bladders—the early ancestors of football pigskins—into the center of the opposing town. There were neither rules nor referees in these often violent encounters. King Henry II (1133–1189) banned the competitions during his reign because of the vandalism and mass homicides that accompanied them.[1] After that, the popular game was played only in places where the participants could bribe the authorities. By the sixteenth century, however, it was reestablished publicly and played on fields with borders and real goalmouths to defend. It eventually morphed into the game of soccer. Some three hundred years later, American college football was born—though it more resembled the sport of rugby than the football we know today—when in 1869 a pair of New Jersey schools, the Rutgers Queensmen (Rutgers University) defeated the New Jersey Tigers (Princeton University) by a score of 6–4 in the city of New Brunswick.[2]

Today the National Football League (NFL) features a trio of teams whose nicknames reflect the game's warring roots: Vikings, Buccaneers, and Raiders.

Minnesota Vikings (1961-present)

© NFL.com

The Vikings received their name because of a strong Nordic heritage in the northern Midwest of the United States, which is populated by many Americans of Danish, Finnish, Icelandic, Norwegian, and Swedish descent. In Norse, *Viking* means "pirate."[3] But the Vikings were more than brutal pirates. They were explorers, warriors, and merchants as well. The Vikings both plundered and colonized the coasts of northern and western Europe between the eighth and eleventh centuries. They possessed advanced sailing and navigational skills and traveled in longboats that used both sails and oars for added speed.[4] The Vikings, though, were generally a nonliterate culture, recording little of their own history in books. Most of what we know about the Vikings comes from other cultures.

The horn emblems that decorate the Minnesota Vikings' football helmets are meant to mirror those once believed to be worn by real Vikings. However, these warriors never actually went into battle with horns on their helmets. Why? Because of the Vikings' close-quarters style of combat, the sharp horns would have caused serious harm to their fellow troops.

In popular culture, Marvel Comics' superhero Thor is based on the Asgardian god of thunder in Norse mythology. Thor's enchanted hammer, *Mjölnir*, grants him incredible powers, including flight and the manipulation of weather. Now wouldn't he enhance the Vikings' chances for a winning football season?

The Minnesota Vikings' fight song, "Skol, Vikings," is also tied to the team's Nordic heritage. *Skol* is a Danish-Norwegian-Swedish word that means "cheers" or "good health," as in a celebratory toast.[5] The song is played at home games whenever the Vikings score a touchdown.

Singer-songwriter Prince (1958–2016), a Minnesota native, also wrote a fight song for the Vikings entitled "Purple and Gold," inspired by their team colors.[6]

To learn more about Vikings, go online and check out the Viking age or Viking longships. You can also research the lives of famous Viking warriors such as Erik the Red and his son Leif Ericsson. And don't forget to listen to Prince's rendition of "Purple and Gold."

Alternative Team Names: Vikes. The Vikings are also referred to as the Purple People Eaters because of their purple uniforms and fearsome defense that swallows up opponents.

Other Teams Named Vikings: Cleveland State (OH) and Portland State (OR)

Tampa Bay Buccaneers (1976–present)

© NFL.com

The Buccaneers get their name from the French word *boucan*, a grill used for smoking the dried meats once served on ships at sea.[7] This basically means buccaneers were among the earliest fans of jerky. During the late seventeenth century, buccaneers were sponsored by England and France to disrupt the rival Spanish shipping industry in the Caribbean. Authors such as Robert Louis Stevenson and Jonathan Swift glorified the adventures of these organized bands of pirates who democratically elected their captains and evenly divided their stolen spoils under the principles of liberty, equality, and fraternity. The crew, not the captain, decided which ships to attack.[8] These buccaneers sailed without pay, growing wealthier only on what they plundered. How much of a team were the early buccaneers? They actually formulated a kind of insurance policy for their shipmates who were injured in battle and couldn't partake in the crew's next raid, ensuring them a cut of the profits. But don't believe the buccaneers were overly kind. They earned a reputation as such fierce fighters that many ships simply surrendered to them. That combination of team spirit and toughness makes Buccaneers a great nickname for a football franchise in Tampa Bay, a harbor city situated on the west central coast of Florida.

Robert Louis Stevenson's *Treasure Island* is a famous tale of buccaneers and buried gold. Check it out from your local library and read about teen Jim Hawkins's adventure aboard the pirate ship *Hispaniola*, as he tries to keep a treasure map from falling into the hands of a one-legged buccaneer named Long John Silver.

The Tampa Bay Buccaneers began by losing the first twenty-six games in their franchise's history, thus giving their own fans that sinking feeling. Not to fret, though. The Buccaneers eventually went on to capture Super Bowl XXXVII in 2002, defeating a fellow war-inspired team named the Oakland Raiders by a score of 48–21. The team currently plays at Raymond James Stadium, which has a 103-foot pirate ship built into it. The ship has a huge skull decorating the bow (front) and eight working cannons. It is manned by a thirty-person crew on game days. Whenever the Buccaneers score, the cannons are fired—six times for a touchdown (6 points), three times for a field goal (3 points), twice for a safety or two-point conversion (2 points), and once for an extra point after a touchdown.

Keeping to a Theme: A pair of Tampa Bay's soccer teams also carried buccaneer/pirate-inspired nicknames. They were the Tampa Bay Rowdies

(1975–1993) and the Tampa Bay Mutiny (1995–2001). A *mutiny* occurs when a faction of shipmates overthrow the captain, seizing control. But since buccaneers elected their captains and could probably call for a revote, a mutiny sounds rather extreme, don't you think?

Alternative Team Name: Bucs

Other Teams Named Buccaneers: The New Orleans Buccaneers played pro hoops in the American Basketball Association (ABA) from 1967 to 1970. Also, the University of the Virgin Islands calls their athletic teams the Buccaneers.

Oakland Raiders (1960–present)

The Oakland Raiders' nickname was ultimately inspired by a marine raider from World War II (1939–1945), who submitted it for a name-the-franchise contest. It wasn't the original winning entry, though. Ownership had decided on a different submission—the Oakland Señors ("mister" or "sir" in Spanish)—but the nickname was suddenly switched prior to the team's beginning play after the press hinted that the contest was rigged.

© NFL.com

The real-life Raiders were part of the United States Marine Corps, an elite fighting force within an elite fighting force. They staged special amphibious or water-related raids behind enemy lines, usually landing on the shore in rubber boats.[9]

The football franchise bearing the Raiders' name developed an image that was just as tough. The battle cry of their fans, who often wave the Jolly Roger (a pirate flag featuring a skull and crossbones), is simply: "Go to War!" On the field the Raiders, clad in silver-and-black uniforms, featured players with nicknames such as "Snake," "Mad Bomber," "Hit Man," and "Dr. Death." In 1978, in a sad and freak occurrence, Raiders defender Jack "The Assassin" Tatum delivered a devastating hit on Darryl Stingley, leaving the New England Patriots receiver a paraplegic and forever searing the Raiders' over-the-top aggressive nature into sports culture.

Images of Raiders in popular culture can be seen in a pair of world-famous video games. In *Call of Duty*, the first level is set on Makin Island with fictionalized members of the legendary 2nd Marine Raiders. *Madden NFL* is named after John Madden, who coached the Oakland Raiders to victory in Super Bowl XI and became even more well known as a TV announcer and sports analyst. The EA Sports game, which first appeared in 1988, has come out with a new edition every year since 1990, selling more than 130 million copies.

And of course there's the 1981 adventure film *Raiders of the Lost Ark*, in which George Lucas and Steven Spielberg introduced the world to Dr. Henry "Indiana" Jones, played by Harrison Ford. Interestingly, the movie is set in the year 1936, six years prior to the advent of the real-life Marine Raiders.

In 2020 the Oakland Raiders are scheduled to move to the city of Las Vegas.

Alternative Team Names: Silver and Black (the team's colors), Men in Black (for the popular 1997 sci-fi film *Men in Black*), Raider Nation, The Black Hole (Raiders defense). The team also went by the name Los Angeles Raiders from 1982 to 1994, when its home games were played in LA.

Other Teams Named Raiders: Colgate University (NY) and Wright State University (OH). Texas Tech University goes by Red Raiders.

Pittsburgh Pirates (1891–present)

In 1889 baseball's Pittsburgh Alleghenies, who played beside the Allegheny River in Pennsylvania, were renamed the Pirates. They were given the nickname after a complaint was lodged against them by another team, accusing the Pittsburgh club of being "piratical" or pirate-like in their signing of a player from the roster of a franchise that had recently folded.[10]

Hall of Famer Honus Wagner played for the Pirates from 1897 to 1917. Due to his superb speed, Wagner was nicknamed "The Flying Dutchman," which is also the name of the legendary ghost pirate ship that can never make port, with the souls upon it doomed to sail the seven seas forever.[11]

Images of the *Flying Dutchman* can be seen in many diverse forums. The ship has appeared in cartoons such as *SpongeBob SquarePants* and *Scooby-Doo*, and was the subject of an opera by German composer Richard Wagner (1813–1883). In literature, Samuel Taylor Coleridge's (1772–1834) famed poem *The Rime of the Ancient Mariner* (1798) features a similar ghost ship inhabiting its stanzas. And in popular film, the *Flying Dutchman* appears in *Pirates of the Caribbean: Dead Man's Chest* (2006).

One Expensive Baseball Card: The Honus Wagner baseball card (T206) is one of the rarest in the world, with fewer than sixty copies known to still be in existence. How did it get so rare? Issued by the American Tobacco Company from 1909 to 1911, the card was given away free with the purchase of its tobacco products. Wagner, however, was a fierce opponent of tobacco and refused to let his card continue in production. So fewer than two hundred cards were ever distributed to the public. In 2007 a T206 Honus Wagner judged to be in near-mint condition sold for $2.8 million, the highest price ever paid for a baseball card.[12]

Alternative Team Names: Bucs and Buccos

East Carolina University Pirates

East Carolina University, located along the Tar River in Greenville, North Carolina, once went by the nickname Teachers because the school trains future educators. But after several seasons of being held scoreless multiple times in football games, the university searched for a name that might evoke more spirit from the student body. The eventual choice was Pirates.

In an incredible coincidence, one of the Carolinas' most famous pirates was an Englishman named Edward Teach. He was better known as Blackbeard the Pirate, who sported a thick black beard as part of his fearsome image. In 1718 Teach perished in a bloody battle with soldiers, several months after running his ship, the *Queen Anne's Revenge*, aground at the entrance to a North Carolina harbor. The price of defeat in those days? Teach's severed head was hung from the conquering ship's bowsprit (the metal or wooden beam extending forward from the front point of the boat).[13]

Other Teams Named Pirates: Hampton University (VA) and Seton Hall University (NJ). There's also pro football's Pittsburgh Pirates (1933–1939), which was once coached by John "Blood" McNally. Now that's a nickname for a pirate!

University of New Orleans Privateers

The University of New Orleans reached back into its city's warring past to choose the nickname Privateers. Unlike pirates, privateers were commissioned by a state to attack enemy ships. They obtained what was known as a letter of marque to make their actions legal and not a hanging offense. Though the crews weren't paid, they were allowed to keep what they seized from other vessels.[14]

During the Battle of New Orleans in January 1815, privateers were vital in securing the city, which sits at the mouth of the Mississippi-Missouri River system, against the powerful British Navy. The most well known of the privateers was Jean Laffite, a Frenchman. During this intense battle versus the British, Laffite aided US forces led by General Andrew Jackson, who later became the seventh president of the United States and is currently pictured on the $20 bill. Laffite's heroics eventually earned him a presidential pardon by James Madison for his past piracy.[15]

Baltimore Bullets (1963–1997)/Washington Wizards (1997–present)

Sporting contests are often described in the media using violent imagery, with words like *whipped*, *slaughtered*, and *destroyed* punctuating the storyline. But in 1997 Baltimore/Washington Bullets owner Abe Pollin decided the name of his pro basketball team was inappropriate for Washington, DC, a city that at the time was suffering from a severe outbreak of gun violence. Pollin was also moved by the assassination of his close friend, Israeli prime minister Yitzhak Rabin. Therefore, the owner renamed his franchise the Washington Wizards.

"Bullets connote killing, violence, death," Pollin told the *New York Times*. "Our slogan used to be 'Faster than a speeding bullet.' This is no longer acceptable."[16]

CHALLENGE #1: LESS VIOLENT LANGUAGE

Welcome to your first challenge! Now that we've properly warmed up, get ready to exercise your brain. Here are your instructions: Grab a sheet of paper and rewrite the following game summary removing the warlike imagery and replacing it with words that carry less violent connotations.

Vikings Slaughter Bucs

The Minnesota Vikings battered the Tampa Bay Buccaneers on Monday Night Football, 40–17. The Buccaneers' defense was assaulted by two first-quarter touchdowns as the Vikings' vaunted passing attack ripped apart the opposition's secondary. Minnesota runners struck for 200 yards on the ground, including a walloping 90-yard touchdown run just before halftime that all but killed the Buccaneers' chances and spirit. The 23-point loss was the worst whipping of the season for the Buccaneers, who had been slapped with a three-touchdown beating in their previous game.

SPORTING PEOPLES

Boston Celtics (1946–present)

The franchise's first owner, Walter Brown, chose the name Celtics because so many people of Irish descent inhabited the city of Boston, Massachusetts. That meant he wanted to fill the stands with paying fans. The Celts (pronounced *kelts*) were various groups of

© NBA.com

people who lived throughout Europe at a time when the Roman Empire was growing. The main trait linking the tribes of Celts was their language, which still has a strong presence today in Scotland, Wales, and Ireland.[17]

Boston's Celtics amazingly won eight consecutive National Basketball Association (NBA) Championships from 1959 through 1966. Now that's a dynasty! Hall of Fame center Bill Russell won eleven titles playing for the Celtics.

Alternative Team Name: Celts
Another Team Named Celtics: Carlow University (PA)

University of Notre Dame Fighting Irish

The University of Notre Dame calls it sports teams the Fighting Irish. In the early nineteenth century, there was a strong anti-Catholic sentiment facing Irish immigrants who had come to the United States. Signs were actually posted at work sites looking to hire that read: "Irish Need Not Apply!" or "Irish Go Home!" The phrase "Fighting Irish" was a slur in New England during this time period. Notre Dame, which is located in South Bend, Indiana, embraced the nickname to represent people who suffered from discrimination.[18]

Alternative Team Names: Irish and Fighting Leprechauns (from their logo)

Edmonton Eskimos (1949–present)

The Edmonton Eskimos of the Canadian Football League (CFL) are named after the indigenous people who have traditionally inhabited the polar regions of Canada, Siberia, Alaska, and Greenland. The term *Eskimo*, though, is often considered insulting and has widely been replaced by *Inuit* or by names specific to particular communities. The Inuit smartly adapted to the harsh and freezing weather of their landscape by relying on fish, sea mammals, and land mammals for their food, clothing, power source, and tools.

Alternative Team Names: Esks, Eskies, and the Double-E
Another Team Named Eskimos: Pro football's Duluth Eskimos (1926–1927)

University of Pennsylvania Quakers

The Quakers first appeared in England during the middle of the seventeenth century. They broke away from the established Church of England and faced strong persecution there. Pennsylvania, which was founded by William Penn in 1682, was intended as a safe place for Quakers to practice their faith.[19] Hence, the University of Pennsylvania refers to its sports teams as the Quakers. One of the things Quakers have contributed to our language is the usage of *thou* as a pronoun, often replacing *you*. For example: "Thou hast [*has*] been gone for a long time."

Other Teams Named Quakers: Guilford College (NC), Earlham College (IN), and Wilmington College (OH)

San Diego State Aztecs

The Aztec Empire refers to certain ethnic groups of central Mexico who dominated the area from the fourteenth through sixteenth centuries. San Diego State chose the nickname to honor the Aztec civilization's qualities of strength, valor, and intellectual achievement. The Aztecs were ingenious farmers who battled the intense heat of their region by building an elaborate system of canals for irrigation.[20] The Aztecs also built steep pyramids with religious temples on top at which to worship. They even created their own calendar in the form of a round sun stone—perhaps the most famous work of Aztec sculpture, weighing nearly twenty-four tons and featuring the face of their sun god.

© iStock/AarStudio

Go online or to your local library to find out about the Aztecs' fierce battles with the Spanish conquistador Hernán Cortés that ultimately changed the balance of power in the region.

Another Team Named Aztecs: Pima Community College (AZ)

Yeshiva University Maccabees

Hanukkah is known as the Festival of Lights, and the Maccabees play an important role in that celebration. In reclaiming their temple after a sustained war against those who wanted to suppress their religious freedom, the Maccabees possessed enough clean oil to burn for only one day. The oil, however, miraculously lasted for eight days. This is why modern menorahs have eight candles, to recognize each day the oil burned. New York's Yeshiva University, a school of Jewish heritage and faith, calls its athletic teams the Maccabees.

University of Hawaii Rainbow Warriors/Rainbow Wahine

When a beautiful rainbow appeared over the stadium during a University of Hawaii football game, the press seized on the image and began calling the team the Rainbows instead of their actual name at the time, the Deans.[21] The colorful nickname caught on.

During the late eighteenth century, King Kamehameha I and his warriors fought to unite the Hawaiian Islands, which include eight major islands and hundreds of smaller ones spread over fifteen hundred miles. In paying homage to the islands' roots, the university added Warriors to the team's nickname, becoming the Rainbow Warriors. *Wahine* is the Hawaiian word for "woman"; correspondingly, the school's women's teams are nicknamed the Rainbow Wahine.

Hawaii is the fiftieth state, giving us the final star on the US flag. It is the only US state outside of North America—rather, it is located in a region of the world called Oceania.

Alternative Team Names: Bows and SandBows (women's team)

2

AMERICAN HISTORY

NATIVE AMERICANS

Washington Redskins (1932-present)

Sports teams named after peoples or aspects of various cultures have become an extremely sensitive issue. Does the name honor the chosen group or does it reduce them to mere mascots, creating an atmosphere of inequality? To this point, the NFL's Washington Redskins have become a true lightning rod for serious debate. The term *redskin* was originally used to describe the scalps that bounty hunters provided as proof of their killings of Native Americans. Initially, little attention was paid to the outcry of Native Americans over this issue. But the decades of the 1960s and 1970s inspired an increase in social awareness, which continues today. Native Americans and other groups contend the name Redskins promotes harmful stereotypes, pointing to examples such as a 1998 headline from the *Washington Post*—"Cowboys Finish Off Redskins."[1] In sharp contrast, representatives of the team have presented the argument that the nickname symbolizes the greatness and strength of native people, appropriately honoring them.

Over the past few decades, the number of teams with names relating to Native American heritage has declined dramatically at the high school and college levels. Universities such as St. John's, Stanford, Dartmouth, and Marquette have all changed their once Native American–inspired nicknames. However, no team at the professional level has yet to switch their name, including baseball's Cleveland Indians and Atlanta Braves, football's Kansas City Chiefs, and hockey's Chicago Blackhawks. Some newspapers even have editorial policies of avoiding all use of their nicknames, limiting references to these teams to their location only.

Collegiate Name Changes: St. John's, once nicknamed the Redmen, became the Red Storm; Stanford changed its moniker from the Indians to the Cardinal (singular color); Dartmouth became the Big Green after similarly ditching Indians; and Marquette dumped the Warriors to be renamed the Golden Eagles.

Atlanta Braves (1996–present)

The baseball organization called the Braves began in the city of Boston during the late nineteenth century, where it experimented with a number of nicknames, waiting for one to catch on with fans. It cycled through names such as the Red Stockings (1871–1875), Red Caps (1876–1882), Beaneaters (1883–1906), Doves (1907–1910), Rustlers (1911), Braves (1912–1935), and Bees (1936–1940). Finally, the fickle franchise settled again on the name Boston Braves (1941–1952) before it left Massachusetts for the state of Wisconsin and became the Milwaukee Braves (1953–1965). More than a decade later the team changed venues again, moving to Georgia as the newly minted Atlanta Braves.

The Braves grew a wide fan base during the late 1970s after the team became a featured attraction on one of the first national cable networks, Turner Broadcasting System (TBS). But that notoriety also drew attention to the franchise's Native American symbols, including mascot Chief Noc-A-Homa (pronounced *knock-a-homer*), who emerged from a teepee in the bleachers and performed a dance whenever a Braves player hit a home run.[2] The character of Chief Noc-A-Homa was eventually retired by the club in 1986.

During the 1991 World Series, Braves owner and media mogul Ted Turner, who also owned TBS, and his then-girlfriend, actress Jane Fonda, came under intense criticism for doing the tomahawk chop from their seats in the stands to support the team. The tomahawk chop, done en masse by fans at the stadium, simulates a throwing motion of a tomahawk (a small Native American hand ax used for building, hunting, and battle), often while holding an oversized foam tomahawk and vocalizing a stereotypical Native chant. The activity sparked protests outside the stadium by opponents who believed the act was demeaning to Native Americans.

Alternative Team Names: Bravos and America's Team (due to their nationwide exposure on TBS)
Other Teams Named Braves: Alcorn State University (MS) and Bradley University (IL); Buffalo Braves (NBA, 1970–1978)

Cleveland Indians (1915-present)

The Cleveland baseball team was once nicknamed the Naps—short for Napoleons. No, not for the French military leader Napoleon Bonaparte (1769–1821), but for Hall of Famer Nap Lajoie, who both played for and managed the squad.[3] This made the Cleveland Naps an eponym, which is when a word in society evolves from someone's name. But when Nap Lajoie left, the franchise was eventually renamed the Indians.

The team's logo—a cartoon version of a grinning, red-faced Indian named Chief Wahoo—has long drawn the ire of Native Americans and others who have protested against it. Over the last decade or so, the team has slowly shifted to featuring other logos on their uniforms instead, including a block letter *C* for Cleveland. In early 2018 Major League Baseball and the Indians organization announced that Chief Wahoo would be removed from the team's uniforms as of the 2019 season.

Major League, a 1989 comedy film starring Charlie Sheen, Tom Berenger, Renee Russo, and Hall of Fame baseball announcer Bob Uecker, features a fictionalized version of the Cleveland Indians.

Alternative Team Names: The Tribe and Wahoos
Other Teams Named Indians: Catawba College (NC), Chipola College (FL); pro football's Buffalo Indians (1940–1941)

Chicago Blackhawks (1926-present)

The Chicago franchise in the National Hockey League (NHL) is named for the 86th Infantry Division, nicknamed the Blackhawk Division, in which their original owner, Frederic McLaughlin, served during World War I. In turn, that infantry division was named for a leader of the Sauk nation called Black Hawk (1767–1838),[4] who actually fought on the side of the British during the War of 1812, hoping to push white settlers out of Sauk lands. He is also credited with writing the first Native American autobiography, entitled *Autobiography of Ma-Ka-Tai-Me-She-Kia-Kiak or Black Hawk, Embracing the Traditions of His Nation*, which was published in 1833.[5]

The NBA's Atlanta Hawks (1968–present) also owe their team's name to Black Hawk. This basketball franchise began as the Tri-City Blackhawks (1946–1951), playing home games in both Illinois and Iowa. After landing in Milwaukee and then St. Louis, the team shortened its moniker to Hawks before finally settling in Atlanta.

Kansas City Chiefs (1963–present)

The Chiefs franchise actually hailed from the land of the celebrated American cowboy, beginning its history as the Dallas Texans (1960–1962). Talk about switching sides. Like an acting extra in an old-fashioned Western movie, the team moved to Missouri and became the Kansas City Chiefs, reflecting that state's heritage and Native American culture. Seven different tribes inhabited Missouri—the Chickasaw, Illini, Ioway, Missouria, Osage, Otoe, and Quapaw. *Missouri* is a native word that means "big canoe people."

Florida State Seminoles and Central Michigan Chippewas

The Florida State Seminoles are named after the courageous Seminoles who inhabit the harsh environment of the Florida Everglades and who refused to be conquered or to surrender their culture.[6] Florida State University has worked diligently with representatives of the Seminole Tribe of Florida to remove any stereotypical symbols, forming a strong bond between the two communities.

Similarly, the Central Michigan Chippewas are the athletic teams representing Central Michigan University. In 2005 the school was placed on the NCAA's list of schools with "hostile or abusive" nicknames. But with the support of the Saginaw Chippewa Indian Tribe, who believed they were being properly honored, the university appealed that decision. Ultimately, the appeal was upheld and the name currently remains in use.

Alternative Team Names: The Seminoles, a boy's name in the tribe's native language, are often called the Noles. Likewise, the Chippewas are sometimes referred to as the Chips.

Oorang Indians (1922–1923)

Many Native Americans played professional football during the first quarter of the twentieth century. The most famous, Jim Thorpe, won both the decathlon (ten separate events scored as one) and pentathlon (five separate events scored as one) at the 1912 Summer Olympics. During the 1922 and 1923 seasons, Thorpe coached and played for a Native American football team in Marion, Ohio, called the Oorang Indians.[7] The Indians' roster included players with names such as Arrowhead, Barrel, Big Bear, Black Bear, Deadeye, Deer Slayer, Joe Little Twig, Red Fang, Red Foot, Red Fox, and Wrinkle Meat.

CHALLENGE #2: DATING THE CENTURY

Historical events are marked by dates and centuries. For example, earlier we learned that the Vikings were a force in Europe from the eighth to eleventh centuries. But how do we know to which century a historical date belongs? It's simple. Let's look at the date 755. Since the first seven hundred years have already been filled up, and we're already heading toward the next hundred—the eighth hundred—the year 755 is part of the eighth century. The year 826 would be part of the ninth century, and so on.

Now that you understand the process, grab a separate sheet of paper and for each of the five dates listed below give the correct century:

1. 912
2. 1389
3. 1755
4. 1965
5. 2014

REVOLUTIONARY TEAMS

Philadelphia 76ers (1963-present)

The NBA's Philadelphia 76ers owe their name to the year in which the United States was born. On July 4, 1776, the Continental Congress adopted the Declaration of Independence. The document, penned by Thomas Jefferson with help from John Adams and Benjamin Franklin, officially separated the thirteen American colonies from Great Britain and outlined the principles by which our new nation would govern itself.

Part of the Preamble to the Declaration of Independence reads, "We hold these truths to be self-evident, that all men are created equal, that they are endowed by their Creator with certain unalienable rights, that among these are life, liberty and the pursuit of happiness."

There are twenty-six known copies of the Declaration of Independence. The most recognized copy resides in Washington, DC, in the National Archives.[8] It is on display inside a specially constructed glass case and is closely guarded.

Alternative Team Name: Sixers

New England Patriots (1960-present)

The New England area—which comprises Connecticut, Maine, Massachusetts, New Hampshire, Rhode Island, and Vermont—was central to the events and battles of the American Revolution. The NFL's New England Patriots boast a nickname that pays homage to the daring individuals of that period who risked their lives for independence. The real-life Patriots were also known as Revolutionaries, Continentals, or American Whigs. They included names from history such as John Adams, Thomas Jefferson, John Hancock, and silversmith Paul Revere.

Alternative Team Name: Pats
Other Teams Named Patriots: George Mason University (VA) and University of the Cumberlands (KY)

New England Tea Men (1978-1980), University of Massachusetts Minutemen, and New England Revolution (1994-present)

The North American Soccer League's New England Tea Men recognized the Sons and Daughters of Liberty who, during the Boston Tea Party of 1773, destroyed crates of tea aboard British ships in Boston Harbor. The incident was a protest over the colonies' being taxed without proper representation in the British government.[9] Similarly, the University of Massachusetts Minutemen are named for the civilian militia that could seemingly be assembled at a minute's notice to fight the Redcoats. The area also sports a Major League Soccer (MLS) team aptly named the New England Revolution.

Charlotte Hornets (1988-2002, 2014-present)

Charlotte, North Carolina, was named after the wife of England's King George III. While occupying the city in 1780, British general Charles Cornwallis received such hostile treatment from the locals that he referred to Charlotte as "a hornet's nest of rebellion."[10] The city even adopted a hornet's nest as its official emblem. The NBA's franchise there is perfectly nicknamed the Charlotte Hornets. Correspondingly, the woman's pro basketball team was named the Charlotte Sting (1997–2007). And the nickname of the arena where both teams played? Why, the Hive, naturally.

Alternative Team Names: Buzz City; from 2004–2014 the NBA's Charlotte franchise played under the nickname Bobcats
Other Teams Named Hornets: Sacramento State University (CA), Kalamazoo College (MI), and Emporia State University (KS)

© NBA.com

US HISTORY 101

San Francisco 49ers (1946–present)

In 1849, "gold fever" struck San Francisco. Gold was discovered in the streams and riverbeds of the Sierra Nevada, east of the city. That's when prospectors, otherwise known as forty-niners, raced across the country to California. The fever was so bad that ships sat abandoned in the local harbor and San Francisco's two newspapers shut down because everyone was out prospecting for gold.[11]

What makes gold so valuable? Well, it's one of the rarest natural resources on earth. Gold conducts electricity better than any other metal. It can easily be shaped into jewelry, while corrosive agents such as oxygen and heat have little effect on its brilliance.[12]

The NFL's San Francisco 49ers are a fitting tribute to that period in US history called the California Gold Rush. And yes, one of the 49ers' outstanding uniform colors is gold.

A line about "a miner, forty-niner" also appears in the lyrics of the western folk song "Oh, My Darling Clementine."

Columbia College in California goes by the nickname Claim Jumpers. That's a person who illegally occupies and mines someone else's land or claim. During the Gold Rush, claim jumpers were the scourge of the West, and hated by legitimate hard-working forty-niners.

Alternative Team Name: Niners

Other Teams Named 49ers: Long Beach State University and the University of North Carolina–Charlotte (because its predecessor school was saved from being shut down in 1949)

Chicago Fire (1997–present)

The MLS's Chicago Fire owe their nickname to a tragic event in Chicago history. In the very dry summer of 1871, a fire broke out beside a barn belonging to a family named O'Leary. Firefighters were sent to the wrong address, and a strong wind quickly spread the blaze throughout the city of mostly wooden structures. The fire burned for two days. Much of Chicago was destroyed, and more than one hundred thousand people were left homeless.[13] Legend has it that Mrs. O'Leary's cow accidentally started the fire by kicking over an oil-burning lantern, making the Great Chicago Fire the first time that a cow was ever used as a scapegoat.

New York Renaissance (1923–1949)

The Harlem Renaissance (1920–1930) marked a period in Harlem, a section of New York City, during which African American writers, musicians, painters, and dancers celebrated and defined their heritage. During this period, however, African Americans athletes were still not allowed to play on professional teams with white athletes. In 1923 the New York Renaissance, an African American basketball team, was formed. The Rens won eighty-eight straight games between 1932 and 1936, defeating many white teams in unofficial contests. The Renaissance, which is a French word for "rebirth," received their name from the Renaissance Ballroom, where they played their home games.[14]

Check out the 2011 documentary on the Rens entitled *On the Shoulders of Giants: The Story of the Greatest Team You Never Heard Of.* The film is cowritten and co-narrated by NBA Hall of Famer Kareem Abdul-Jabbar.

Also, go online to research the lives and work of Harlem Renaissance artists such as dancers Josephine Baker and Bill "Bojangles" Robinson, writers Langston Hughes and James Baldwin, and musicians Louis Armstrong and Ella Fitzgerald.

University of Oklahoma Sooners

The University of Oklahoma's teams are nicknamed the Sooners. Why? In 1899, Congress opened up almost 2 million acres for settlers. It was referred to

as the Land Run of 1899 because when official permission was given, the settlers raced onto the land to claim the best plots. However, close to ten thousand
homesteaders near Oklahoma Station entered the area too soon and hid in the
countryside. Once the run officially began, they jumped out to stake their claims
ahead of the rest. Hence, we have the Oklahoma Sooners.[15] You can view a
depiction of this in the 1992 movie *Far and Away*, starring Tom Cruise and
Nicole Kidman.

Philadelphia Eagles (1933–present)

When the NFL's Philadelphia Eagles came into existence, the United States was
in the midst of the Great Depression that began in 1929. The Great Depression
was a severe worldwide economic downturn. Here in the United States, there
was a terrible stock market crash. Many Americans lost their jobs and were
unable to support their families. In an effort to provide work and relief for
Americans, President Franklin D. Roosevelt introduced the New Deal program
through the National Recovery Administration. That put many Americans to
work building roads and dams. The National Recovery Administration had an
eagle as its symbol, inspiring the newly born Philadelphia football franchise to
choose the nickname Eagles.

For the 1943 season the Pittsburgh Steelers and Philadelphia Eagles combined rosters, calling themselves the Phil-Pitt Steagles. The short-lived union
happened because both teams lost many players to military service during
World War II.

Alternative Team Names: The Birds and Iggles
Other Teams Named Eagles: Approximately
   forty-five teams, including Bridgewater Col-
   lege (VA), Georgia Southern University, Cop-
   pin State University (MD), Emory University
   (GA), Alabama Southern, Ashland University
   (OH), Florida Gulf Coast University, and
   American University (Washington, DC)

© NFL.com

LITERATURE, LANGUAGE, AND MYTHOLOGY

LITERARY INFLUENCES

Baltimore Ravens (1996–present)

The Baltimore Ravens of the NFL owe their name to the great American short story and mystery writer Edgar Allan Poe (1809–1849), who in 1845 published a dark narrative poem called "The Raven":

© NFL.com

> Once upon a midnight dreary, while I pondered, weak and weary,
> Over many a quaint and curious volume of forgotten lore—
> While I nodded, nearly napping, suddenly there came a tapping,
> As of some one gently rapping, rapping at my chamber door.
> "'Tis some visitor," I muttered, "tapping at my chamber door—
> Only this and nothing more."

Poe's narrator, who is grief-stricken by the death of his love, named Lenore, is visited by a mysterious talking raven. The hopelessness that the narrator feels is reinforced by the one word the ominous bird can speak—"Nevermore."

In 1849 Poe died in in the city of Baltimore. He is buried there, and his gravesite has become a well-visited tourist spot, furthering the bond between the writer and the city, which eventually adopted the name Ravens for its NFL team.

Interested in spooky stories by Edgar Allen Poe? Visit your local library to find a collection of Poe's stories, and check out "The Pit and the Pendulum" and "The Telltale Heart"—if you think you have the courage to get through them.

While you're reading "The Raven," find the line that helped the Baltimore Ravens choose purple as their uniform color. Also, check out *The Simpsons* Halloween episode "Treehouse of Horror I," which contains a parody of Poe's famous poem. Bart Simpson plays the raven, but instead of saying "Nevermore," this raven utters Bart's memorable catchphrase "Eat my shorts."

University of Xavier Musketeers

The Three Musketeers (1844) is a novel by French writer Alexandre Dumas. It is about a young man named D'Artagnan who travels to Paris to join the Musketeers of the Guard, a unit of legendary swordsmen who safeguard the life of the king. He meets the three famous Musketeers of the day: Athos, Porthos, and Aramis. It is a story of friendship, teamwork, and chivalry—a code of conduct for knights and soldiers who dedicated themselves to glory and love. The University of Xavier, which is in Cincinnati, Ohio, adopted the nickname Musketeers for its sports teams. Their mascot is even a Musketeer swordsman named D'Artagnan. It is a perfect fit for a school with ties to the early explorers of the Ohio region from French Canada.[1]

Go to your local library to check out a copy of Dumas's *Three Musketeers*. Perhaps you've heard the Musketeers famed motto of teamwork: "One for all, and all for one."

Mudville Nine (1984)

The Mudville Nine, a former minor-league baseball team in Stockton, California, received its name from Ernest Lawrence Thayer's "Casey at the Bat" (1888). The famed poem, which is part of baseball lore, details the defeat of the fictitious Casey, who plays for the home team, described as the "Mudville Nine." Casey comes to bat in the final inning with his team trailing by two runs. There are two outs and two runners on base. Casey represents the winning run. He is so confident in his abilities that Casey passes on the first two pitches, both called *strikes*, without ever lifting the bat off his shoulder. Then, on the final pitch, the overconfident Casey swings and misses, disappointing his town and team.

The poem concludes with these lines:

and somewhere men are laughing, and somewhere children shout;
but there is no joy in Mudville—mighty Casey has struck out.

In 1996 actor James Earl Jones, who is the voice of Darth Vader from *Star Wars*, recorded the poem. Singer John Fogerty in his 1985 hit song "Centerfield" alludes to Casey striking out.

Boston Bruins (1924–present)

The NHL's Boston Bruins, one of the league's Original Six franchises, owes its name to the medieval fables about Reynard the Fox, which contain a character named Bruin the Bear.[2] *Bruin* was a term used for a brown European bear. Its origins can be traced back to the fifteenth-century middle-Dutch words *bruyn* and *bruun*.[3] The fable is a medieval allegory, in which symbolic animal characters take the place of people to deliver a broader message. An example of a famous allegory in literature is George Orwell's novel *Animal Farm* (1945), with animals substituting for political figures.

Alternative Team Name: Killer B's
Other Teams Named Bruins: University of California at Los Angeles and Belmont University (TN)

Hitting the Books: If you truly like literary inspiration in the nicknames of your athletic teams, few will outdo *Los Libros* (Spanish for "the books") of Saint John's College in New Mexico. That's almost as good as a librarian named Paige. Can't you just hear the opposing football coach's speech to his players: "I want you all to hit the Books really hard this week."

Brampton Excelsiors (1883–present)

In Latin, *excelsior* means "higher." This word was particularly inspirational to an educator named George M. Lee at Brampton High School in Brampton, Ontario. He'd experienced it in Henry Wadsworth Longfellow's poem "Excelsior," about a young man climbing a mountain through harsh circumstances and refusing to relinquish a flag with *Excelsior* written upon it:[4]

A traveler, by the faithful hound,
Half-buried in the snow was found,
Still grasping in his hand of ice
That banner with the strange device,
  Excelsior!

So when Lee began a box lacrosse team (played indoors), he named it the Excelsior Lacrosse Club, which has been a mainstay on the Canadian sports scene for more than 135 years. And that number of years, as well as the impact on the Excelsiors' athletes and many fans, will only grow higher.

In the United States, the state of New York also recognizes great value in the ideals of striving to reach higher, prominently displaying the word "Excelsior" on its state flag.

Whittier College Poets

Athletes at Whittier College are nicknamed the Poets. Yes, even the football team. The Whittier College Poets are named in honor of Quaker poet John Greenleaf Whittier. The school itself is named after him, as is the city in which it is located, Whittier, California. Whittier was also an abolitionist—someone who advocated for the abolishment of slavery.[5]

Former US president Richard Milhous Nixon (1913–1994) was a member of the football team at Whittier College, though he admittedly spent most of the time on the bench.

CHALLENGE #3: ROMAN NUMERALS AND THE SUPER BOWL

The Super Bowl, the NFL's championship game, is tracked using Roman numerals—a system in which letters are used to represent numbers. The San Francisco 49ers won Super Bowl XVI in 1981 and Super Bowl XIX in 1984. So how do we turn those letters into actual numbers? Well, the X represents the number 10, the V represents the number 5, and I singularly represents the numbers 1 through 3 (I is 1, II is 2, and III is 3). Here's the trick, though: We can never use more than III in a row. That means the number 4 is represented by IV (1 less than 5 equals 4) and 9 is represented by IX (1 less than 10 equals 9).

The 49ers won Super Bowl XVI (10 + 5 + 1 = Super Bowl 16) and XIX (10 + 9 = Super Bowl 19).

Here's your question: The 49ers also went on to win Super Bowl XXIII, Super Bowl XXIV, and Super Bowl XXIX. What number Super Bowls do those Roman numerals represent?

SPORTING LANGUAGE

Los Angeles Dodgers (1958–present)

Major League Baseball's Los Angeles Dodgers aren't named for the Artful Dodger from Charles Dickens's novel *Oliver Twist*, or even because the city is big on the sport of dodgeball. The Dodgers actually started out playing in Brooklyn, where trolley cars were once part of New York City's mass transit system, rolling above ground through the streets. So the dodgers are actually trolley dodgers—ducking out of the way of the passing cars.[6]

© iStock/PictureLake

Jackie Robinson broke baseball's color barrier when he took the field for the Brooklyn Dodgers in 1947, becoming MLB's first African American player and effectively ending racial segregation in baseball, which had plagued the major leagues for six decades. Robinson's struggles and achievements were the subject of a movie entitled *42*, which was the number on his uniform. Today, no other baseball player is allowed to wear that number. That all changes, however, on baseball's annual Jackie Robinson Day, when every player on every team wears number 42 in his honor.

Georgetown University Hoyas

Georgetown University is located in Washington, DC. The university's athletic teams are nicknamed the Hoyas, and the school uses a bulldog as its mascot. A Hoya, however, is not a canine. It seems Georgetown's teams were originally called the Stonewalls. In cheering for their classmates, students studying Greek and Latin started chanting *Hoya Saxa*, meaning "What Rocks." Eventually, the name from the chant replaced the old nickname, giving birth to the Georgetown Hoyas.[7]

Fun Fact: The name Super Bowl was inspired by a children's toy. Lamar Hunt, who at the time owned football's Kansas City Chiefs, saw his son playing with a Super Ball—a solid rubber ball that could bounce several stories high. Most of the big season-ending games in college football had the word *Bowl* attached to them—the Orange Bowl, Sugar Bowl, Rose Bowl, and Cotton Bowl. That combination of factors lead Hunt to coin the name Super Bowl. That name, however, was slow to be adopted. The first season-ending meeting between the American Football League (AFL) and its rival National Football League was called the AFL-NFL World Championship.[8] It was played in January 1967 in Los Angeles, where the Green Bay Packers defeated Hunt's Chiefs by a score of 35–10. It wasn't until the third contest, in 1969, when the New York Jets defeated the Baltimore Colts, 16–7, that the championship game officially bore the title Super Bowl.

Montreal Expos (1969–2004)

When the Montreal Expos franchise was born, the owners needed to satisfy two audiences in the French Canadian city—one that spoke English and one that spoke French. They were initially focused on calling the team the Royals because the city of Montreal takes its name from Mt. Royal. But the fledgling team from Kansas City, which entered Major League Baseball in the same year, adopted the name Royals first. After much deliberation, the franchise finally chose Expos, which is spelled the same way in both English and French.[9] The name was inspired by the Expo '67, a World's Fair and International Exposition held in Montreal two years earlier.

Alternative Team Names: Spos and *Nos Amours* ("Our Love" in French)

Louisville Bats (2002–present) and Altoona Curve (1998–present)

Hitters pick up bats and pitchers often throw curveballs to fool them. The minor-league Louisville Bats are nicknamed in honor of Louisville Slugger, a Louisville, Kentucky–based company that has made wooden baseball bats since 1884. The Altoona Curve, another minor-league squad, is named after a huge curve of railroad track in Altoona, Pennsylvania. The curve—which is nearly twenty-five hundred feet long and thirteen hundred feet in diameter—is used to lessen the grade or climb up to the summit of the Alleghany Mountains.[10]

I know you've heard of batboys and batgirls, young people who bring loose bats back to baseball dugouts. But the Trenton Thunder, another minor-league franchise, has replaced batboys and batgirls with bat-fetching dogs. Better not laugh too hard. You may be replaced next. How so? The Hanwha Eagles of

South Korea baseball are introducing Fanbots to take the place of live fans in the stands. Go online to witness both bat-fetching dogs and Fanbots.

Purdue University Boilermakers

I suppose the athletic teams at Purdue University should be grateful. After their football team thrashed an interstate rival's team—a 44–0 drubbing near the end of the nineteenth century—students and fans of that overwhelmed school began shouting insults at Purdue's players, making fun of their large size. Imagine shaming football players for being too big and powerful? A local news headline from that town read: *Slaughter of Innocents . . . by the burly boiler makers of Purdue.*[11] The nickname Boilermakers stuck. It was a reference to boilers on steam-powered locomotives. These trains were usually powered by burning coal or wood, which superheated the water in a boiler, producing steam to power the train's pistons, which were attached to the locomotive's wheels.

In the kid's TV show *Thomas the Tank Engine and Friends*, Thomas is a steam-powered locomotive.

WORDPLAY

Here is a quartet of teams whose names spring from the evolution of our ever-changing English language.

New York Knicks (1946–present)

The NBA's Knicks—short for Knickerbockers—received their nickname from the term used to refer to early Dutch settlers of the 1600s in New York. *Knickers* were a style of knee-length trousers worn by men and boys during this era. The writer Washington Irving even used Knickerbocker as a pen name for his 1809 book *A History of New York*. Then, in the late nineteenth century, a newspaper cartoon featured a character called Father Knickerbocker—dressed in a cotton wig, three-cornered hat, buckled shoes, and, of course, knickers—who became an early symbol of New

York City. When the New York Knicks were born, they adopted the character of Father Knickerbocker, pictured dribbling a basketball, as their first logo.[12] The team's name was a fitting choice considering that basketball players wear shorts while playing.

New York Yankees (1913–present)

© MLB.com

During the American Revolution (1775–1783), *Yankee* was a derogatory term used by the British toward natives of the American colonies. British redcoats even began singing a marching tune, "Yankee Doodle Dandy," to mock the American forces who fought in their work clothes instead of military uniforms. But with each victory over their British counterparts, the colonialists began to adopt the word as a source of pride.[13] A century later, Southern Confederates used the same term to refer to Northerners, or those in the Union, during the American Civil War (1861–1865).

Yankee also refers to those living in New England, which comprises the states of Connecticut, Maine, Massachusetts, New Hampshire, Rhode Island, and Vermont. Author Mark Twain penned a book called *A Connecticut Yankee in King Arthur's Court*, about a man transported back in time. The main character uses modern technology to fool the people of the Early Middle Ages into believing he is a great magician. Twain himself practiced a little bit of deception over his own name. Mark Twain is actually a pen name taken from his time as a riverboat pilot on the Mississippi; it means the water is two fathoms (or twelve feet) deep, a safe depth for a steamboat to pass. His real name was Samuel Clemens.

Despite fielding some of the greatest baseball players of all time—including Babe Ruth, Lou Gehrig, Mickey Mantle, and Derek Jeter—the Yankees are one of only two professional sports franchise that do not feature the players' names across the back of their uniforms. That's because the name across the front—Yankees—is supposed to be more important, blending individual players into a team unit.

Alternative Team Names: Yanks, Pinstripers (for their pinstriped uniforms), and the Bronx Bombers (because Yankee Stadium is located in the Bronx, one of the five boroughs of New York City).

Other Teams Named Yankees: Football's New York Yankees (1946–1949) also played their home games in the Bronx's Yankee Stadium; the Boston Yanks (1944–1948), also of pro football, competed at Fenway Park in Boston.

Interesting Dilemma: If New Englanders are actually Yankees—and the city of Boston, Massachusetts, is part of New England—how can fans of the Boston Red Sox despise their bitter rivals the New York Yankees so much? Aren't they really despising themselves?

Dallas Mavericks (1980–present)

An eponym is a word that was once someone's proper name. That's how the Dallas Mavericks of the NBA received their nickname. Samuel Augustus Maverick (1803–1870), a Texas land baron and legislator, once owned a herd of cattle to which he didn't pay particular attention. Over time, the new calves born to that herd went unbranded. Neighboring ranchers began to recognize and refer to those unmarked calves as "Mavericks."[14] Today, mavericks are either horses (like the mustangs of the American West) or bovines that live in the wild. People can also be referred to as mavericks. In this case, a maverick is anyone who displays independent thoughts or actions, a nonconformist.

© NBA.com

Alternative Team Name: Mavs
Other Teams Nicknamed Mavericks: Minnesota State University, Colorado Mesa University, University of Nebraska–Omaha, and University of Texas–Arlington

University of North Carolina Tar Heels

The University of North Carolina's sports teams are called the Tar Heels. Basketball great Michael Jordan is one of the school's most famous alumni. Tar was once a major product and export of North Carolina. During the American Civil War, a regiment of soldiers from the state stuck to their positions so fiercely during a battle, it was joked that they had tar on their heels. The name Tar Heel, however, was also used as an insult, suggesting that poorer residents of North Carolina, who walked around barefoot, had tar-stained heels to show for it.[15]

Tar is a black or dark brown viscous and sticky liquid that can be produced from coal, wood, petroleum, or peat.[16] One of its main uses in Colonial America was to protect the wooden frames of ships from rotting. Today, tar is more likely to be used to seal a roof from moisture. Asphalt is a naturally occurring type of tar or *pitch* often used for paving roads.

One of the most well-known natural producers of tar is the La Brea Tar Pits in Los Angeles, California. These pits have supplied us with many perfectly preserved mammal fossils, including those of mammoths and saber-toothed cats. Animals would wander into the pits and become stuck, then predators, looking to feed upon them, would enter and become stuck in the viscous substance themselves.

The Blacktop: Street basketball is often said to be played on the blacktop. That's because the outdoor basketball courts of many parks and schoolyards are covered and sealed with black asphalt.
Alternative Team Name: Heels

Fun Fact: Besides basketball's Mavericks, there are many other examples of eponyms in modern language. There is the month of July—inspired by Julius Caesar, who ruled the Roman Empire from 44–49 BCE; Thursday (Thor's Day)—named after the Norse god of thunder; and Achilles' heel—named after the Greek hero Achilles, whose one vulnerable spot was his heel. The word *odyssey* springs from a character in mythology named Odysseus, who took a long and eventful journey. (We'll learn more about him in the next section.) In sports, the Zamboni, which resurfaces the ice at hockey games, was named after its inventor, Frank J. Zamboni.

MYTHOLOGY

Toronto Argonauts (1873-present)

The Toronto Argonauts of the CFL, the oldest professional football team in North America, derive their nickname from a famous story in Greek mythology. The Argonauts were a band of fifty heroes who accompanied Jason aboard the ship *Argo* on his quest to fetch the Golden Fleece, sometime before the Trojan War. The most famous of these heroes was Hercules.

© TorontoArgonauts.com

The Argonauts sports franchise traces its roots back to the late nineteenth century when the Argonaut Rowing Club formed a football team, hence the connection with heroics on the sea. Inspired by the colors of the rowing teams at both the University of Oxford (dark blue) and the University of Cambridge (light blue) in England, the Argonauts chose double-blue, a combination of dark and light blue, as their colors.[17] Because of the Argonauts' popularity, other Toronto-based sports teams—including hockey's Toronto Maple Leafs and baseball's Toronto Blue Jays—were also inspired to adopt the color blue. And like the Blue Jays, the University of Toronto Varsity Blues bear this theme in their nickname.

Alternative Team Name: Argos; Boatmen or Scullers (both rowing terms)
Canada's Title Game: The CFL's equivalent of the Super Bowl is called the Grey Cup, and as of 2018 the Toronto Argonauts have been crowned champions a record seventeen times since the game's inception in 1909.

Tennessee Titans (1999–present)

The name Titans springs from Greek mythology. The Titans were the second generation of divine beings. Their leader was Cronus, who overthrew his parents Uranus (Father Sky) and Gaia (Mother Earth). Cronus in turn was defeated by his own son, Zeus, in the War of the Titans.

Thus the NFL's Tennessee Titans are a team whose nickname fits their home city of Nashville perfectly. Why? Nashville is often referred to as "The Athens of the South" because of its many universities (Vanderbilt, Tennessee State, Belmont, and Fisk) and classical architecture, much like the ancient Greek center of learning. There is even a life-sized replica of the Greek Parthenon in Nashville.[18]

The original Parthenon, a temple of the Greek goddess Athena, was built in the fifth century BCE. It still stands today at the Acropolis in Athens, Greece, and is recognized as one of the world's great cultural monuments. You can go online to learn more about Greek architecture, best known for its theaters and temples to gods such as Zeus, Apollo, and Poseidon.

Titans of New York/New York Jets (1959–present) and New York Giants (1925–present)

The NFL's New York Jets (1962–present) were originally nicknamed the Titans of New York (1959–1962). That's because their established crosstown football rivals were the New York Giants. In Greek mythology, the Titans battled against the Giants, who were human in appearance but generally greater in stature and strength.

Why did the Titans of New York change their name to Jets? Well, they began playing their home games at Shea Stadium, which was situated next to LaGuardia Airport. The stadium was directly in the path of hundreds of daily flights, constantly flying overhead.

Titans in Popular Culture: In the series Percy Jackson and the Olympians by author Rick Riordan, the Titans play the role of villains who attempt to rule the world once more after escaping from their underworld prison. In the biographical sports film *Remember the Titans* (2000), the Titans are the nickname of the integrated Virginia high school football team that overcame both internal and external prejudices during the early 1970s. DC Comics even has a fictional teenage team of superheroes called the Teen Titans.

Alternative Team Names: The New York Jets are often referred to as Gang Green because of their uniform color. The New York Giants are also called the G-Men and Big Blue (also for their uniform color).

Other Teams Nicknamed Titans: Cal State Fullerton, University of Detroit Mercy, and Illinois Wesleyan

Other Teams Nicknamed Giants: San Francisco Giants (baseball) and Yomiuri Giants (Japanese baseball)

Another Team Nicknamed Jets: Winnipeg Jets (hockey)

Canisius College Golden Griffins

The Canisius Golden Griffins represent the athletic teams of Canisius College in Buffalo, New York. Griffins are mythological creatures sporting the body of a lion and the head of a bird, usually an eagle. They historically perform a protective function and first appeared in ancient Middle Eastern and Mediterranean cultures in the second millennium BCE.[19]

In the Harry Potter series by J. K. Rowling, Gryffindor were champions at Quidditch, a made-up game now being played for real at some schools. Pictured on the Gryffindor crest is a lion, no doubt inspired by the griffins of mythology.

Jiangsu Pegasus (2005–present)

This member franchise of the China Baseball League is nicknamed for the winged stallion Pegasus of Greek mythology. Legend says that everywhere the horse stuck his hoof to the earth, a spring of water came forth. Pegasus is also known as a source of inspiration to poets.

Where can you currently find Pegasus? Just study the stars tonight. There is a constellation named for him in the northern sky. Mythology tells us that Zeus, who is king of the gods, magically transformed the horse, placing him amid the heavens to shine forever. Mirroring that, the Jiangsu Pegasus were formerly nicknamed the Hopestars.

Avenging Rivals: The image of the superhero is dominant in modern mythology. Here are a group of athletic teams that certainly could stand up against any Marvel Comics or DC Comics supervillains, at least on the playing field: the St. Francis Xavier University X-Men and X-Women in Antigonish, Nova Scotia; the University of Iowa Hawkeyes; the ASA College Avengers in New York City; and pro basketball's Pittsburgh Ironmen (1946–1947).

Elon University Phoenix

In 1923, Elon University in North Carolina was devastated by a raging fire. Like the mythical phoenix, the school reemerged stronger from its own ashes. That's why their athletic teams are named Phoenix.

Every five hundred years, when it feels its death approaching, the phoenix supposedly builds a nest in an oak tree. Coincidentally, in Hebrew, *elon* means "oak." The phoenix's legendary colors are maroon or crimson and gold, the same as those worn by Elon's athletic teams.[20]

In the Harry Potter series, Fawkes, Albus Dumbledore's defender and companion, is a crimson-and-gold phoenix that eventually bursts into flames.

University of Southern California Trojans and Michigan State Spartans

On the college football field, who would win a game between the University of Southern California Trojans and the Michigan State Spartans? Why, Greek mythology assures us the Spartans would triumph, of course! They have a sweet trick play called the Trojan horse. Homer was a Greek poet who lived in the eighth century BCE. According to his epic poem *The Odyssey*, twenty-five Spartans, led by Odysseus, hid inside the hollowed-out stomach of a huge wooden horse. The horse was left at the gates of Troy as the symbol of the Trojans' victory over the Greeks in a long, bitter war. Once inside the city, the Spartans snuck out under cover of night and burned the city full of drunken Trojan soldiers who believed the war was over.

You can witness the Trojan War played out on the big screen in the 2004 film *Troy*, starring Brad Pitt.

Other Teams Nicknamed Trojans: University of Arkansas at Little Rock, Troy University (AL), Virginia State University, Seminole State University (OK), and Mount Olive College (NC)

Other Teams Nicknamed Spartans: Norfolk State University (VA), University of North Carolina at Greensboro, San Jose State University (CA), and University of Tampa (FL)

4

MUSIC AND
POP CULTURE

RHYTHM AND FLOW

The sport of basketball was invented by Dr. James Naismith in Springfield, Massachusetts, in 1891. The first goals (rims) were a pair of peach baskets nailed to the balcony railing of a local gym. The game was originally intended to keep football players in shape during the winter months. Instead of today's 5-on-5, it was a very crowded 9-on-9. Originally, the baskets didn't have the bottoms cut out. Every time a goal was scored, a janitor had to come out with a ladder to retrieve the soccer-style ball from the basket.[1] How were the early shooting percentages? Not so good. There was more discord on the court than in the rhythmically flowing sport we know today. The first game ever played ended with a score of only 1–0.

Cleveland Rockers (1997–2003)

Cleveland, Ohio, is home to the Rock and Roll Hall of Fame. The city was one of the first to embrace the music billed as rock and roll in the early 1950s by a Cleveland disc jockey and record store owner named Alan Freed.[2] Its amplified sound, which inspired the same movement in an audience as passengers rocking and rolling aboard a ship at sea, helped to make the electric guitar and bass important instruments. Today, this style of music is more commonly called simply *rock*. In honor of Cleveland's connection to this music, the city's former Women's National Basketball Association (WNBA) franchise was aptly named the Cleveland Rockers.

New Orleans/Utah Jazz (1974–present)

Since the time Naismith invented the game, basketball teams have been searching for their scoring rhythm. The names of some fran- chises, however, put themselves squarely ahead of the competition in this regard. The NBA's New Orleans Jazz honored that city's musical heritage with its nickname. The birthplace of jazz, the port city of New Orleans is where Eu- ropean, African, Caribbean, West Indian, and other musical influences fused to create a new sound at the turn of the twentieth century.[3] Jazz is difficult to define, but it often contains elements of improvisation (unplanned or inventing at the moment), which opens the doors to different musical possibilities during every performance.

In 1980 the New Orleans Jazz relocated to Salt Lake City, Utah, more than fourteen hundred miles away. Did the franchise choose a new nickname to re- flect the team's new surroundings—perhaps one inspired by Utah's sensational skiing, snowfall, or mountain ranges? No way. Instead, they left fans with one of the most mystifying monikers in all of sports—the Utah Jazz.

St. Louis Blues (1967–present)

The NHL's St. Louis Blues owe their name to that city's relationship with a style of music referred to as the blues. Blues lyrics usually talk about personal suf- fering and lost love. W. C. Handy, who is often called the Father of the Blues, wrote his famous 1914 song *St. Louis Blues* after a chance meeting with a woman on the streets there who was distraught over her runaway husband.[4]

You can go online to hear blues legends such as Ella Fitzgerald, Nat King Cole, Cab Calloway, and even W. C. Handy himself perform rousing renditions of *St. Louis Blues*.

Philadelphia Soul (2004–present)

The Philadelphia Soul of the Arena Football League team is named after the confluence of soul music that flowed from the Philadelphia area throughout the decades of the 1960s and 1970s. It has been called "The Sound of Phila- delphia" or simply TSOP, which was also the title of a hit record in 1974 by MSFB. One of the football Soul's original co-owners was musician Jon Bon

Jovi. Several of the recording artists associated with the Philly Soul Sound are Teddy Pendergrass, Hall and Oates, Patti LaBelle, Instant Funk, O'Jays, and the Tramps. You can go online to check out MSFB's recording of "TSOP."

New Orleans Saints (1967–present)

The NFL's New Orleans Saints owe their nickname to the American gospel hymn "When the Saints Go Marching In," also known as "The Saints":

© NFL.com

> Oh, when the saints go marching in
> Oh, when the saints go marching in
> Oh Lord I want to be in that number
> When the saints go marching in

The song became a New Orleans jazz standard and is so associated with the city that it became a perfect moniker for the football team. Adding to that, the franchise was adopted into the NFL on November 1, 1966—All Saints Day.[5]

The city of New Orleans was founded by the French in 1718. The Saints' logo is a fleur-de-lis or "flower of the lily," which is an early symbol of French royalty.

In 2005, as Hurricane Katrina devastated New Orleans, residents who couldn't leave the area sought shelter in the Superdome, the Saints' home field, where a section of the roof actually sheared off. In their first home game after the storm, the Saints delivered an emotionally charged victory in front of a national audience on *Monday Night Football*, providing their city with a prideful celebration of rebirth.

Ain't Happening: After enduring decades of futility on the field, Saints fans began calling their team the Ain'ts. Fans even wore paper bags over the heads in the stands. That changed forever in 2010, though, when the Saints defeated the Indianapolis Colts, 31–17, in Super Bowl XLIV for their first championship.
Alternative Team Names: Who Dats (from a chant by their fans) and the Ain'ts
Other Teams Named Saints: Early in the franchise's history, the Chicago White Sox competed as the Saint Paul Saints (1894–1899); also, Siena College (NY), Aquinas College (MI), Ashford University (CA), and Carroll College (MT)

Nashville Sounds (1978–present)

The minor-league Nashville Sounds baseball team receives its nickname from the fact that Nashville, Tennessee, is considered to be the home of country music, and from the 1950s subgenre of country music actually named "The Nashville Sound," which included more polished background vocals and more choruses or refrains—the repeating lyrics in a song.[6] This was done in an attempt to compete with a new style of music that was sweeping the nation: rock and roll. Nashville is also home to the Grand Ole Opry (a weekly concert and worldwide radio show), the Country Music Hall of Fame, and Music Row—a downtown section of music industry offices.

Center Ice/Center Stage: West Side Story is a famous musical inspired by Shakespeare's tragic play *Romeo and Juliet*. These modern star-crossed lovers are named Tony and Maria. It's set on the Upper West Side of New York City in the 1950s. Interestingly, hockey's version of *West Side Story* occurs whenever the San Jose Sharks face off against the Winnipeg Jets. Do you know why? Well, the teams' nicknames mirror the names of the two rival gangs in the musical—the Sharks and the Jets.

CHALLENGE #4: INVENTING A NEW SPORT OR GAME

We have already learned that Dr. James Naismith invented the game of basketball, and we have seen that author J. K. Rowling invented the fictional game of Quidditch for her Harry Potter series. Have you or your friends ever invented your own game? If so, grab a sheet of paper and briefly describe it. If not, why not put your mind to the test and invent one right now? What's the goal of the game? Are there any special rules? How many players per side? What kind of equipment do you need? How much space is required to play? Is it played indoors or outdoors? Make a drawing of the playing field. Now that we know something about how sports teams get their nicknames, what name might you give a team to play this new game? And why would that name be appropriate?

THAT'S ENTERTAINMENT

Los Angeles Lakers (1960–present)

The NBA's Los Angeles Lakers have an alternative nickname—Showtime. It's inspired by both their legendary fast-breaking offense, once led by Earvin

"Magic" Johnson, and Hollywood's movie and entertainment industry, which supplies many stars sitting courtside watching the team play. But how did they get the name Lakers? Well, after the 1959 season, the franchise moved west from its original home of Minneapolis, Minnesota. The state of Minnesota is known as the Land of 10,000 Lakes. To be precise, it has 11,842 lakes of ten acres or more.[7] Those lakes were formed during the last Ice Age, when glaciers moved back and forth across most of Minnesota, which is a Dakota Indian word meaning "sky tinted waters."[8]

Other Teams Named Lakers: Grand Valley State University (MI), Lake Superior State University (MI), and the State University of New York–Oswego

Anaheim Ducks (2007–present)

© NHL.com

It's not often that life imitates art. But that's exactly how hockey's Disney-owned Mighty Ducks of Anaheim came to be. In 1992 Disney had a hit movie entitled *The Mighty Ducks*, about a pee-wee hockey team of misfits searching for their confidence. The box office success of the film spawned the real-life team, which is today known simply as the Anaheim Ducks. What do fans call the arena where the Ducks skate? Why, the Pond, of course.

Another Team Named Ducks: University of Oregon

Orlando Magic (1989–present)

Disney influenced another pro sports team's name. The NBA's Orlando Magic is no Mickey Mouse franchise. However, it does owe its nickname to Disney World's Magic Kingdom, which opened in 1971 and is located in nearby Bay Lake, Florida. A number of fans in a name-the-franchise contest submitted Magic before it ultimately became the winner among the finalist names, which also included Tropics, Juice, and Heat.[9]

The Magic Kingdom, which is dedicated to fairy tales and Disney characters, is the world's most visited theme park, routinely drawing more than 20 million visitors per year.[10] It is home to Cinderella Castle (based on the castle seen in the 1950 film *Cinderella*) and Main Street USA. Its slogan is "The Most Magical Place on Earth."

Harlem Globetrotters (1926–present)

Also known as the Clown Princes of Basketball because of their great showmanship and on-court comedy routines, the perfectly nicknamed Globetrotters have circled the globe countless times, playing more than twenty thousand exhibition games in 120 countries. The Globetrotters have won more than 98 percent of those games. The team began in Chicago, Illinois, as the Savoy Big Five, playing exhibitions in the Savoy Ballroom before big dances.[11] Among the Globetrotters' most famous players are Meadowlark Lemon, Herbert "Geese" Ausbie, and Wilt Chamberlain, who once scored one hundred points in an NBA game. The Globetrotters longtime opponent and comedic foil has been the Washington Generals.

Interestingly, the Globetrotters had little connection to Harlem. The name was selected by their ownership because Harlem (a section of Manhattan in New York City) was considered to be the center of African American culture. The team had competed for forty-two years before they ever actually played a game in Harlem in 1968.[12]

Unclamped: The Miami Vise of the Arena Football League played but one game in their franchise history. The team was named after the TV series *Miami Vice*, about two undercover Miami detectives, Sonny Crockett and Rico Tubbs, who drove a Ferrari Daytona and Testarossa. Now that's going undercover in style! The show, known for its trendsetting fashions, aired from 1984 to 1989, winning over more fans than their football counterpart.

The Dream Team (1992)

The 1992 Summer Olympics in Barcelona, Spain, were dominated by the US men's basketball squad, which earned the nickname "The Dream Team." It was the first time that professional NBA players competed for the United States in the Olympics. Naturally, they were a nightmare for opposing countries. The Dream Team went undefeated en route to winning a gold medal, beating their opponents by an average of forty-four points per game. And the truth is that it was more of a spectacle than competitive hoops.

The Dream Team defeated Cuba by a score of 136–57. In response to the drubbing, Cuba's coach, Miguel Calderon Gomez, was quoted as saying, "You can't cover the sun with your finger."[13]

The US squad was comprised of pros Larry Bird, Michael Jordan, Charles Barkley, Magic Johnson, Patrick Ewing, Karl Malone, John Stockton, Clyde Drexler, Chris Mullin, Scottie Pippin, and David Robinson. All of them have made it to the NBA Hall of Fame. The only amateur/collegiate on the team was Christian Laettner of Duke. The head coach was Chuck Daly, who guided the Detroit Pistons to a pair of NBA Championships.

Durham Bulls (1902–present)

© DurahmBulls.com

The film *Bull Durham* (1987), starring Kevin Costner, Susan Sarandon, and Tim Robbins, featured real-life minor-league baseball team the Durham Bulls. The North Carolina–based franchise began in 1902 as the Durham Tobacconists, recognizing the state's tobacco industry.[14] They were renamed the Bulls in 1913, eventually playing in El Toro Park with a real bull as a mascot. The film's famous snorting bull prop, which was built for the movie, has remained ever since, becoming a fixture at Durham Bulls home games. The sign attached to it reads, "Hit Bull, Win Steak." The current bull is 20 feet tall, 30 feet wide, approximately 10 feet off the ground and 310 feet away from the batter, beyond the left-field fence.[15]

Springfield Isotopes

The Springfield Isotopes are the fictional baseball team on *The Simpsons*, the longest-running sitcom in US history, which debuted in 1989. Thirteen different US states have cities called Springfield. However, the series has never pinpointed exactly which one is home to Homer, Marge, Bart, Lisa, and Maggie Simpson. Now, what's an isotope? Better get out your chemistry book. An isotope is any of two or more forms of an element having the same atomic number but different atomic weights. On the animated series, Springfield's economic hub is a nuclear power plant owned by Homer Simpson's boss, Montgomery C. Burns. So it's quite a fitting nickname for the team.

Northwest Arkansas Naturals (2008–present)

The Naturals, a minor-league baseball franchise, owe their name to a pair of inspirations. The first is the 1984 baseball film *The Natural*, featuring actor Robert Redford as Roy Hobbs, a possibly past-his-prime member of the New

Box Office Sports: Over the years, fictionalized sports teams have been a big part of filmmaking and carrying a story line. Teams featured in movies often become an additional character, which the audience roots either for or against. For example, in the *Longest Yard* (1974), Burt Reynolds played a former pro quarterback and current inmate on a prison football team nicknamed the Mean Machine, which did battle against the prison's guards. Why did it feel so real? Reynolds once played college football for the Florida State Seminoles.

Here is a list of other such teams and their films:

- The cartoon Monstars competed against Michael Jordan, Bugs Bunny, Daffy Duck, and other Looney Tunes in *Space Jam* (1996).
- The Miami Sharks took to the gridiron with actor Al Pacino portraying their head coach in *Any Given Sunday* (1999).
- *The Bad News Bears* (1976) naturally featured a Little League baseball team called the Bears, which Walter Matthau managed in the character of Morris Buttermaker, an ex-pro pitcher and part-time swimming pool cleaner.
- Paul Newman took to the ice in the hockey movie *Slap Shot* (1977), skating for the minor-league Charlestown Chiefs.
- The Average Joes were the likable dodgeball team in the Ben Stiller/Vince Vaughn vehicle *Dodgeball: A True Underdog Story* (2004).
- In *Semi-Pro* (2008), Will Ferrell portrayed Jackie Moon, the owner/player/coach of a Flint, Michigan–based basketball team called the Tropics, which was trying to make the leap from the folding ABA to the NBA.

York Knights baseball team. The film is based on the superb novel of the same title penned by Bernard Malamud. The second is the fact that Arkansas is nicknamed "The Natural State." Known for its incredible scenic beauty, Arkansas is home to three national forests and five national parks. The state also sports the first nationally protected river—the Buffalo River, which is one of the few remaining undammed rivers in the United States.[16]

FIRST OFFICIAL TIMEOUT: CREATING YOUR OWN HOME TEAM

Here's our first official timeout.

Now that you've gotten a firsthand look at how sports teams get their nicknames, it's time to create one yourself. You can begin by doing it close to home, where you're very familiar with the surroundings. You now have the opportunity to create a brand-new sports team for your city or state, including its all-important nickname.

Here are some things to keep in mind when choosing an inspiration for a name: Does your city have any outstanding physical features (such as being located on the shore or mountains)? Is it well known for any specific foods? Does its populace have any special occupations? Is it known for any distinct kinds of weather events, or wildlife or plant life? These details can all be of great help in creating a nickname. Remember, your team doesn't have to play one of the major sports, such as baseball, football, basketball, hockey, or soccer. You can choose a name for a track team, bowling team, swimming team, math team (they're called mathletes), debate team, or almost anything else for which you have a competitive passion.

Now grab a sheet of paper and create a team deed. Be sure to include your name as owner, your team's home city or state, the sport your team will play, and its all-important nickname. Also, explain how you chose your team's nickname.

5

CHANGING SOCIETY: GENDER AND RACE

GIRL POWER

All-American Girls Professional Baseball League (1943–1954), Women's United Soccer Association (2001–2003), and National Women's Football League (2000–present)

Over the past half century, the names given to women's sports teams have changed dramatically. In the early 1940s, The All-American Girls Professional Baseball League was founded by chewing gum mogul Philip K. Wrigley, who was worried that World War II would draft all of professional baseball's best players for soldiers. However, Wrigley also believed the public would accept only female athletes who projected soft, nonthreatening images. So he sent his players to charm school and made sure they received tips on fixing their hair and makeup. Forget about long pants for sliding; Wrigley had his players competing in fashionable skirts raised several inches above the knee.[1] The nicknames of the teams—which included the Racine Belles, Rockford Peaches, Grand Rapids Chicks, Fort Wayne Daisies, Muskegon Lassies, and Chicago Colleens—also followed suit.

A fictionalized version of the lives of these groundbreaking women athletes can be seen in the 1992 film *A League of Their Own*, which centers around two sisters playing for the rival Racine Belles and Rockford Peaches.

Now fast forward to the Women's World Cup soccer final in 1999. Wrigley surely would have swallowed his chewing gum as the US's Brandi Chastain, who had just scored the winning goal against China, whipped off her jersey, celebrating in a black sports bra in front of more than ninety thousand fans in attendance and millions more watching on TV. The success of the US team paved the way for the Women's United Soccer Association, the first pro soccer league for women. The new league boasted franchises with noticeably stronger nicknames, including the New York Power, Carolina Courage, and Boston Breakers.

At the start of the twenty-first century, women wearing shoulder pads took on a whole new meaning with the formation of several professional football leagues for females. Many of the teams' nicknames—such as the Connecticut Crushers, St. Louis Slam, West Michigan Mayhem, and Keystone Assault—reflected the true bone-jarring nature of the sport.

Los Angeles Amazons (2002-present)

Football players are known for their size and strength, which is why the Los Angeles Amazons of the Independent Women's Football League are perfectly named. In Greek mythology, the Amazons were a nation of all-female warriors who carried swords and shields. DC Comic book superhero Wonder Woman (cre-ated in 1941) is an Amazon princess who came to life after being sculpted from clay by her mother, Queen Hippolyta. Hippolyta also appears as a character in William Shakespeare's comedy *A Midsummer Night's Dream*. In fact, one of the earliest mentions of football comes in Shakespeare's tragedy *King Lear*, when the character Kent insults someone by calling him a "base football player."

Fun Fact: You've undoubtedly heard of the Super Bowl. Well, how's this for a gender bender? The championship football game of the National Women's Football Association was called the SupHer Bowl. In 2001, the Philadelphia Liberty Belles, wonderfully named after their city's symbol of freedom, the Liberty Bell, pounded the Pensacola Power, 40–7, to win the inaugural SupHer Bowl. Fittingly, one of the teams competing for the title that season was the Biloxi Herricanes.

New York Liberty (1997-present)

The WNBA features a franchise named the New York Liberty, in honor of the Statue of Liberty in New York Harbor. The statue was a gift from France. It's modeled after Libertas, the Roman goddess of freedom who held a torch and a tablet. Concerned about Lady Liberty's green complexion? That's patina, a type of tarnish (oxidation) that covers surfaces made of copper (like some US pennies). Standing slightly taller than 151 feet in height, Lady Liberty should have no trouble dunking on a regulation 10-foot-high basketball rim.[2]

© WNBA.com

The NHL's Tampa Bay Lightning owe their nickname to central Florida's Lightning Alley, where more lightning strikes occur than anywhere else in the United States, with as many as fifty strikes per square mile each year. But in 1992 lightning stuck in a different way as female goalie Manon Rheaume became the first woman to compete against men in professional hockey when she played in a pair of preseason contests.[3] Though Rheaume never played in a regular-season NHL game, she did win a silver medal in the 1998 Olympics for the Canadian women's team. Her autobiography is aptly titled *Alone in Front of the Net.*

Interested in learning about the lives of other women athletes who broke gender barriers by competing against men on a professional level? Go online to research the lives of basketball player Ann Meyers, baseball pitcher Ila Borders, and football placekicker Katie Hnida.

Portland Thorns (2012–present)

Back in the 1940s, the Portland Thorns would probably have been named the Rose Petals. But not today. The Thorns, a franchise in the National Women's Soccer League, were given a fitting nickname to play in Portland, Oregon, which is known as the Rose City. In the late nineteenth century, the Portland Rose Society planted some twenty miles of Portland's streets with roses.[4] That was to celebrate an upcoming centennial (one-hundred-year anniversary) of the area's settlement by the great explorers Meriwether Lewis and William Clark, who were helped immensely by a native female guide named Sacagawea. The first Rose Festival in Portland was held in 1907, and it continues annually.

Fun Fact: Many colleges have traditionally placed "Lady" before the names of their sports teams when referring to their women's squads. This practice has led to some illogical monikers such as the Massachusetts Lady Minutemen and the St. Peter's Lady Peacocks (females of the species are actually called *peahens*). But other schools have solved this problem beautifully. Northland College's men's teams are named the Lumberjacks, while their women's teams are called the Lumberjills. Syracuse University's teams, once known as the Orangemen, are now simply called the Orange, representing both sexes equally.

Women on US Currency: Both explorer Sacagawea and suffragette Susan B. Anthony appear on their own version of US $1 coins. So far, Martha Washington and Pocahontas are the only women to appear on US paper notes.[5] There has been much speculation, however, that abolitionist Harriet Tubman will adorn a bill in the near future.

CHALLENGE #5: A GENDER-NEUTRAL TEAM NAME

Imagine that your school's sports teams are nicknamed the Anchormen because your school is located near a port on a river. Its logo is a drawing of four muscle-bound males on a ship, hoisting an anchor out of the water. However, many students at your school, especially the female athletes, think this name and logo should be changed. The school newspaper is asking for possible solutions. What are your thoughts? Could you suggest a new nickname or logo? On a separate sheet of paper, brainstorm several possible new nicknames for your school's athletic teams. Remember that your school is located near a river and a shipping port. Using ideas and images that relate to your location would make your suggestions stronger and more relatable. Also, don't forget to draw a new logo.

BASEBALL'S COLOR BARRIER

Baseball's Negro Leagues fielded teams from 1867 until 1962, before and even after baseball became desegregated when Jackie Robinson joined the Brooklyn Dodgers in 1947. Hall of Fame players such as Satchel Paige of the Kansas City Monarchs, Josh Gibson of the Pittsburgh Crawfords, and Hank Aaron of the Indianapolis Clowns played in these leagues.

Pittsburgh Crawfords (1931–1940)

The Crawford Bath House, a recreation center in the Crawford neighborhood of Pittsburgh's Hill District, was the inspiration for the Crawfords' nickname.[6] The Crawfords were originally formed as an interracial club, but as the team became more successful and gained wider recognition, it was forced to segregate. Also known as the Craws, they played their home games at Greenlee Field, one of the few venues owned and built by a Negro League team. Besides Josh Gibson, the Pittsburgh Crawfords fielded Hall of Famers William "Judy" Johnson and James "Cool Papa" Bell.

Indianapolis Clowns (1930–1955)

The Clowns were one of the teams that barnstormed, traveling from city to city to play games for substantial crowds. Like the Harlem Globetrotters of basketball, the Clowns used showmanship and comedy in their approach to baseball—hence the nickname Clowns. The club even fielded the first female professional baseball player to compete against men, Toni "Tomboy" Stone, who played second base for the Clowns in 1953.[7]

A 1976 film entitled *The Bingo Long Traveling All-Stars & Motor Kings* is loosely based on the Clowns baseball team. Besides showing the fun and excitement of baseball, the film also explores many of the roadblocks that a traveling team of African American players had to endure during the 1930s. The film was inspired by the 1973 novel of the same name written by William Brashler.

Genuine or Original Cuban Giants (1885–1915)

The Genuine or Original Cuban Giants were based in Newark, New Jersey. Despite their nickname, they began with no Cubans on the team, though they did play winter baseball in Cuba their first two years of existence, between 1885 and 1887. The club's promoter chose the name to appeal to a wider audience after the Cuban Giants, who were entirely African American, defeated many all-white baseball teams.[8]

Zulu Cannibal Giants (1934–1937)

The Zulu Cannibal Giants, a barnstorming all-black baseball team that infused comedy routines into their play on the diamond, called Louisville, Kentucky, home. The team caused great debate in American society by competing shirtless in grass skirts and with war paint on their faces. Those images played upon the country's worst stereotypes of African Americans. The term *Zulu* refers to an ethnic group of southern and South Africa.

Shade of Difference: Some Negro League clubs used the designation "Black" in front of their nicknames, often to separate themselves from the teams of Major League Baseball. These teams included the New York Black Yankees (1931–1948), Washington Black Senators (1938), Birmingham Black Barons (1920–1960), Baltimore Black Sox (1916–1933), Chattanooga Black Outlooks (1920–1927), and Atlanta Black Crackers (1919–1952).

HURTLING SOCIAL OBSTACLES

Philadelphia SPHAs (1917–1953)

The SPHAs were an acronym—an abbreviation used as a word. SPHAs stood for the South Philadelphia Hebrew Association, which had an all-star basketball team that featured primarily Jewish players. From 1933 to 1946, the SPHAs were a dominant force in the American Basketball League, winning seven championships during that span. Throughout their history, the team endured many anti-Semitic remarks from the press and opposing fans who contended that the SPHAs' Jewish heritage somehow made them genetically superior to play the game of basketball.

Before the SPHAs disbanded in 1959, for a brief time they changed their name to the Washington Generals, in recognition of President Dwight D. Eisenhower, who was also a five-star general. During this period, the team toured as the nightly opponent for the comedic basketball routines of the Harlem Globetrotters.[9]

Springboks (1891–present)

The Springboks are the South Africa national rugby union team. The squad was forced to miss the 1987 and 1991 World Cups because of the world's strong condemnation of South African apartheid, a system of racial segregation authorized by the government. Through political and economic pressure, apartheid came to an end in South Africa in the early 1990s, and in 1994 the country held its first inclusive election, electing Nelson Mandela its president. In 1995 South Africa hosted the World Cup, and the Springboks' victory in the championship match helped to unite many black and white communities who cheered the team with the slogan, "One Team. One Country."

A springbok is a medium-sized antelope native to southern and southwestern Africa. The springbok is known for its *pronking*—making multiple stiff-legged leaps into the air that can reach heights of six feet.

The film *Invictus* (2009) is a dramatization of the Springboks victory in the 1995 World Cup and the squad's influence on rebuilding national pride in South Africa.

Texas Western College Miners

The 1965–1966 Miners of Texas Western College (now the University of Texas at El Paso) were the first team with an all-black starting lineup to win the NCAA University Division Tournament, now known as the NCAA Men's Basketball Tournament. After the Miners defeated the Kentucky Wildcats, who had an all-white starting lineup, they endured many slights that other champions had not. After the game, no one brought out a ladder for the Miners to cut down the nets, so one of their players hoisted another into the air to do so. The team was also not invited onto *The Ed Sullivan Show*, a popular variety show of the era, to take a bow in front of the entire country, as other championship teams had been. The victory had a great impact on American culture because it occurred during the height of the nation's civil rights movement.

The Miners receive their name from the tin mines surrounding El Paso, as well as the city's legacy of processing mined ores from Mexico.

The 2006 film *Glory Road* dramatizes the Miners' victory over the Wildcats, as well as the social obstacles the team encountered along the way.

6

THE NATURAL WORLD

LIONS, TIGERS, AND BEARS—OH, MY!

Detroit Tigers (1901-present) and Detroit Lions (1934-present)

A pair of professional sports teams from the city of Detroit, Michigan, share a common theme—being named for jungle predators. Baseball's Detroit Tigers were named for a military unit called the Detroit Light Guard, which played a significant role in battles during the American Civil War (1861–1865) and the Spanish-American War (1898). That military unit sported the nickname "Tigers." The name was adopted, with permission, by the fledgling baseball team.[1] Three decades later, football's Detroit Lions, hoping to become kings of the NFL jungle, chose their name with great pride. In fact, a group of lions is called a *pride*. Lions are very social animals. An average-sized pride usually consists of several lionesses, their cubs of both sexes, and two adult male lions.

Author and journalist George Plimpton wrote a fascinating nonfiction book called *Paper Lion*, published in 1966. Though he wasn't a pro athlete, Plimpton went to training camp with the 1963 Detroit Lions, where he practiced at quarterback against his rough-and-tumble teammates, who cut him little to no slack. His goal was to "take a snap" against the Cleveland Browns in the Lions' first preseason contest. However, NFL Commissioner Pete Rozelle put a stop to it during the game itself, refusing to let Plimpton step onto the field.

Alternative Team Names: Bengals, Motor City Kitties, and Tigs
Other Teams Named Tigers: Hanshin Tigers (Japanese baseball), Beijing Tigers (Chinese baseball), Auburn University (AL), Clemson University (SC),

DePauw University (IN), Grambling State University (LA), Louisiana State University, Memphis University (TN), Towson University (MD), Princeton University (NJ), and University of Missouri
Other Teams Named Lions: Seibu Lions (Japanese baseball), Tianjin Lions (Chinese baseball), Columbia University (NY), and Loyola Marymount University (CA)

Cincinnati Bengals (1968–present)

Cincinnati, Ohio, is known for its world-class zoo. At the time the city's new football team came into existence, one of the zoo's most famous residents was a rare white Bengal tiger. That gave birth to the tiger-striped Cincinnati Bengals.[2] The Bengal tiger is the national animal of both India and Bangladesh. Unlike lions, tigers are solitary animals who prefer to live alone. Tigers are currently on the list of endangered species. The biggest threats to their existence are shrinking habitats (wildlands being replaced by cities) and poachers, who illegally hunt tigers for their skins and body parts. It has been reported that as few as thirty-two hundred tigers exist in the wild today.[3]

You can go online and search endangered species to see a list of the animals that are facing extinction and what you might be able to do to help save them.

Other Teams Named Bengals: Buffalo State College (NY), Idaho State University, and University of Maine–Fort Kent

Chicago Cubs (1874–present) and Chicago Bears (1919–present)

The NFL's Chicago Bears chose their name as a practical matter. They began playing their games in Wrigley Field, the home of the very popular baseball team the Chicago Cubs. The football team considered adopting the name Cubs as well, but since football players are generally much bigger than baseball players, they smartly chose the nickname Bears instead.[4] How would real bears do on the football field? Though adult grizzly bears can tip the scales at over 550 pounds, they can still run at speeds of nearly 35 MPH. In comparison, top human Olympic sprinters have achieved speeds of 28 MPH.[5]

Prior to 1902 the Chicago Cubs had played under several nicknames: White Stockings (1876–1889), Colts (1890–1897), and Orphans (1898–1902). The

Chicago Daily News is responsible for calling the team the Cubs.[6] The franchise was once owned by former major-league pitcher Albert Spalding, who went on to found the sporting goods company Spalding.

Much to the delight of lifelong Cubs fans, the team ended a 108-year drought between championships when they won the World Series in 2016. Their previous titles came in 1907 and 1908. You can go online to hear singer/songwriter Steve Goodman's "A Dying Cubs Fan's Last Request," about the pain of rooting for a team which hadn't won in so long.

Alternative Team Names: The Chicago Bears are also referred to as Da Bears (inspired by a *Saturday Night Live* comedy skit) and the Monsters of the Midway (originally borrowed from the University of Chicago football team). The Cubs are also called the Cubbies, Northsiders (because Wrigley Field, their home ballpark, is on the North Side of Chicago), Small Bears, and Lovable Losers.

Other Teams Named Bears: Baylor University (TX), Brown University (RI), Mercer University (GA), and Shawnee State University (OH)

Memphis Grizzlies (2001–present)

The NBA's Memphis Grizzlies had their original home in the Canadian city of Vancouver, British Columbia, where they played from 1995 until 2001. The franchise's first choice of a nickname was the Mounties, recognizing the achievements of the famed Royal Canadian Mounted Police (RCMP), who have defended the laws of Canada since 1920. The elite officers often did that on horseback, which is where the word *mounted* comes from in their title. The RCMP, however, objected to the name, so Grizzlies was chosen instead.[7]

Among the Grizzlies uniform colors is Beale Street Blue, a shade named after Beale Street, a famous attraction in Memphis, Tennessee, where blues music took root in the early 1900s.

Fun Fact: The sports teams from the University of California, Los Angeles are referred to as the UCLA Bruins. That choice of nickname shouldn't be surprising. California's state flag, called the Bear Flag, prominently features a large California grizzly bear striding forward on all fours.

© iStock/YangYin

CHALLENGE #6: DEAR POACHERS . . .

While walking through a wildlife preserve, your group discovers a camp left behind by poachers. You see bullet casings and the bones of some animals. The poachers were illegally hunting on that protected piece of land. Your guide takes photos and reports the camp to the authorities. But you decide to leave behind a letter to those poachers. With what we learned in this chapter about endangered animals such as the tiger, what might your letter to them say? Grab a separate sheet of paper and draft a letter to them.

Dear Poachers . . .

WILD STYLE

Minnesota Timberwolves (1989-present)

There hadn't been an NBA franchise in Minnesota since the Lakers moved from Minneapolis to Los Angeles in 1960—until the Timberwolves were born more than three decades later. Minnesota has been vitally important in keeping the wolf population alive in the United States. As their name suggests, timber wolves inhabit wooded areas, something the state of Minnesota boasts in large quantities. For a time, Minnesota actually sheltered the last remaining wild wolves in the United States, except for those in Alaska.[8] Federal laws were passed to protect the wolves, and their numbers have steadily increased. Wolves are part of the canine family, the same as dogs. They howl to communicate with each other, and it is not uncommon for wolves to answer humans imitating their howls.

Alternative Team Name: Wolves

Can't Trust Cartoons: The Arizona Coyotes (1996–present) of the NHL play hockey. Both California State University, Bakersfield, and the University of Texas at San Antonio are the Roadrunners. From watching Wile E. Coyote being left in the Roadrunner's cartoon dust—*Beep! Beep!*—one would believe that roadrunners are faster than coyotes. Yet this is definitely not true. A roadrunner's top speed is approximately 20 MPH, while sprinting. A coyote, though, can achieve speeds of just over 40 MPH. Conclusion? Don't believe what you see in cartoons.

Other Teams Named Timberwolves: Northwood University (MI) and University of Northern British Columbia (Canada); the University of New Mexico is nicknamed the Lobos, which means *wolves* in Spanish.

University of Michigan Wolverines

Before Michigan became a state in 1837, Ohio tried to claim a section of its land. Michigan sent an armed force to discourage some three hundred Ohio soldiers from securing it. The enraged Michigan militiamen chased the Ohio soldiers back to their home state, and even shot at them. Eventually, Michigan was forced to relinquish that tract of land as part of a deal to gain statehood. People from Ohio called Michigan inhabitants Wolverines—the ugliest, meanest, fiercest creatures from the north.[9] That insult turned into a point of pride for those from Michigan. That's why the University of Michigan calls its athletic teams Wolverines.

© iStock/Denja1

Though you may be familiar with the character of Wolverine from Marvel's *X-Men*, a wolverine is actually a stocky, muscular carnivore. It is part of the weasel family, but it looks more like a small bear. A solitary (preferring to live alone) animal, the wolverine can be ferocious in hunting larger animals and possesses great strength in proportion to its size. (No, metal blades don't pop out of its front paws.)

Alternative Team Name: Blue and Maize
Other Teams Named Wolverines: Grove City College (PA), Utah Valley University, and Wesley College (DE)

University of Wisconsin Badgers

Badgers are small nocturnal (active mostly at night) animals with short, powerful legs for digging. They take shelter underground for safety, living in burrows called *setts*. They mostly eat insects, earthworms, and grubs. Wisconsin is called the Badger State. How did that come about? In the first half of the nineteenth century, miners came to Wisconsin to dig for minerals such as lead. During the first brutal winter there, these miners didn't have enough shelters. So they burrowed into the hillsides for protection from the elements, much as badgers do. That spawned the connection, which was eventually embraced by the people of Wisconsin. A badger and miner even appear on the state's official seal.[10] Naturally, the University of Wisconsin calls its athletic teams the Badgers.

Other Teams Named Badgers: Brock University (Canada), Johnson State College (VT), Spring Hill College (AL), and Snow College (UT)

Nashville Predators (1998–present)

The NHL's Nashville Predators first revealed their logo, the fierce head of a saber-toothed cat, and then asked their fans to submit suggestions for a nickname to fit it. The finalists chosen from fans' submissions were Ice Tigers, Fury, and Attack. Then, at the last minute, the team's ownership added their own choice—Predators—into the mix.[11] Is anyone really surprised that ownership's creation won out?

Alternative Team Name: Preds

HOME ON THE RANGE

University of Colorado Buffaloes

In 1934, a University of Colorado campus newspaper ran a contest, and Buffaloes was selected as the nickname for the school's athletic teams.[12] American bison—commonly referred to as buffalo—once roamed the grasslands of North America in huge herds. It is estimated that there were once 60 million, but during the nineteenth century, commercial hunting and slaughter nearly drove them to extinction. But thanks to several national parks and reserve lands, the American bison is now increasing in numbers. An estimated 360,000 are thriving today.[13]

The American bison, or buffalo, is a member of the bovine family, which also includes cows, bulls, and other types of cattle. Why is Buffaloes a great nickname for athletes? Well, buffalo possess great agility and speed (running between 35–40 MPH). Combined with their great size and weight (slightly more than two thousand pounds), a herd of buffalo can be very difficult to stop or contain.

Alternative Team Name: Buffs
Other Teams Named Buffaloes: Arkansas Baptist College, West Texas A&M University, and Milligan College (TN)

Buffalo Bills (1960–present)

In a city called Buffalo, how could the animal of the same name *not* be involved in the moniker of its NFL franchise? After all, its residents are even called Buffalonians. The city in western New York might have received its name from nearby Buffalo Creek, where real-life bison (buffaloes) are thought to have once drank and grazed on grasslands. Previously, in the 1920s, the city had a football team called the Bisons. The new franchise, however, was looking to establish its own identity. The Buffalo Bills adopted the name of a famous barbershop quartet from the area. A barbershop quartet is a vocal harmony group comprised of four singers (a lead singer, a tenor, a bass, and a baritone). They harmonize in a style called *a cappella*, or without musical accompaniment.[14]

The name Buffalo Bills also has a connection to the famed Wild West showman Buffalo Bill Cody, who reportedly hunted and killed more than four thousand bison. Cody was also a rider with the Pony Express, the nation's first mail service. Via train then horseback, the Pony Express boasted of making letter deliveries between New York and San Francisco in only ten days.[15]

Arizona Diamondbacks (1998–present)

Nicknamed after the western diamondback rattlesnake, a venomous species that inhabits the range, grasslands, and deserts of the southwestern United States and Mexico, MLB's Arizona Diamondbacks call the city of Phoenix home. Venomous diamondback rattlers are usually responsible for the greatest number of yearly snakebite fatalities in the United States. Except during mating season, they are solitary reptiles, preferring to live and hunt alone. During the winter months, they hibernate, or brumate—go into a lethargic state—in caves or burrows. Their prey includes prairie dogs, gophers, rats, and mice. Diamondbacks in turn, are hunted by raptors, such as hawks or eagles. The rattling noise produced by the tips of their tails is meant to scare off foes before the snake is forced to strike. The gray-brown-colored diamondbacks are recognized by the distinctive diamond-shaped patterned skin.[16] And considering that baseball is played on a diamond, the Arizona Diamondbacks appear aptly named.

Alternative Team Names: D-Backs, Snakes, and Rattlesnakes

Los Angeles Rams (1936–present [suspended operations for 1943])

Rams are male sheep with horns. Why do they make such a perfect nickname for a football team? Because rams lower their heads and charge each other to assert dominance, exactly like football players on the line of scrimmage. Of course, scientists now know that repeated blows to the head not only cause concussions—when the brain actually makes contact with the skull—but eventually chronic traumatic encephalopathy, which can seriously alter behavior, mood, and thinking.[17] This has led to rule changes and new protective protocols in several sports, but most noticeably football, where tacklers are no longer allowed to lead with the crown of their helmets.

Besides playing in Los Angeles from 1946 to 1994 and 2016 to the present, the Rams have also called Cleveland (1936–1942, 1944–1945) and St. Louis (1995–2015) home.

Alternative Team Names: Fearsome Foursome (the 1960s defensive front line) and Greatest Show on Turf

Other Teams Named Rams: Fordham University (NY), Colorado State University, Winston-Salem State University (NC), University of Rhode Island, and Virginia Commonwealth University

LIKE CATS AND DOGS

Carolina Panthers (1995–present)

It's obvious why so many team nicknames are inspired by felines (cats) and canines (dogs) of all shapes and sizes. They sport the essential qualities that athletes aspire to emulate. Among these qualities are speed, strength, endurance, superior balance, and a highly competitive nature.

The NFL's Carolina Panthers—based in Charlotte, North Carolina—according to Mark Richardson, the original owner's son, received their nickname because "it signifies what we thought a (football) team should be—powerful, sleek and strong."[18]

The Carolina Panthers' logo is of a black panther. It is believed that coloring is a definite advantage for real-life panthers, making them harder to see while hunting in dense forests with lower levels of light.[19]

© iStock/Freder

A black panther named Bagheera is featured in *The Jungle Book* (1894), a collection of stories by author Rudyard Kipling, which has inspired several movies of the same title.

Other Teams Named Panthers: Florida Panthers (hockey); University of Pittsburgh (PA), Adelphi University (NY), Chaffey College (CA), Drury University (MO), Eastern Illinois University, Florida International University, Northern Iowa University, and Virginia Union University are among approximately thirty college athletic teams nicknamed Panthers.

Jacksonville Jaguars (1995–present)

The jaguar is the third largest feline; only the tiger and lion are bigger. The cat's striking appearance—yellow coloring with black spots, or rosettes—is actually a type of camouflage to increase this predator's ability to hunt prey. In the United States, jaguars mostly inhabit the southwestern states.[20] So why did the city of Jacksonville, Florida—which has no jaguars roaming around its outskirts—choose this nickname? At the time of the team's inception, the oldest living jaguar in captivity resided in the Jacksonville Zoo. Another reason was for the sound of the double *J* in the team's name. Both Jacksonville and Jaguars begin with the letter *J*. That interesting and pleasing sound is called *alliteration*.

Alternative Team Name: Jags

Other Teams Named Jaguars: Augusta University (GA), University of South Alabama, and Spelman College (GA)

Two of a Kind: Both the University of Kentucky Wildcats and the University of Arizona Wildcats received their nicknames in identical fashion. The names were inspired by their football teams, who were praised in the press for performing "like wildcats" and winning important games approximately a century (a hundred years) ago.

University of Connecticut Huskies and University of Washington Huskies

Huskies are the world's fastest sled dogs, featuring a strong and compact body type. They are both energetic and athletic, and are the primary breed used throughout the northern regions in sled dog races. Huskies sport a thick double coat of fur and can withstand temperatures as low as -76 degrees Fahrenheit. Their large snowshoe-like feet help them to grip the frozen terrain.[21]

Plenty of working huskies inhabit the Yukon in Canada. Interestingly enough, Yukon is pronounced exactly the same as UConn, the abbreviation for the University of Connecticut, which uses the nickname Huskies for its athletic teams.

The northwestern state of Washington is considered to be the gateway to the Alaskan frontier. Recognizing the importance of the breed to that region, the University of Washington also calls its teams the Huskies.

Balto was a hero husky. The dog led his sled team on the final leg of the serum run to Nome, Alaska, in 1925, delivering an antitoxin to cure an outbreak of a disease called *diphtheria*. There is a statue of Balto in New York's Central Park, and his achievement is celebrated annually by a sled dog event called the Iditarod, an Alaskan race that takes more than a week to complete.[22]

Other Teams Named Huskies: Northeastern University (MA), Northern Illinois University, St. Cloud State University (MN), University of Saskatchewan (Canada), and University of Southern Maine

Nose for the Job: A breed of dog called a bloodhound is well known for its ability to track people by their scent. After sniffing an article of someone's clothing, a bloodhound can track that person for miles. The canines have found missing children, injured hikers on mountainsides, and even escaped inmates from prisons. That's exactly why New York City's John Jay College of Criminal Justice Bloodhounds are so beautifully nicknamed. *Woof!*

Yale University Bulldogs and University of Georgia Bulldogs

Yale, located in the state of Connecticut, has the distinction of being the first school to ever sport a mascot. That tradition began in 1889 and continues today. The mascot's name is Handsome Dan, and he is, of course, a real-life bulldog. The original Handsome Dan was bought by a member of the football team from a local blacksmith for $5. That canine was such a perfect specimen of the bulldog breed, he went on to win more than one hundred prizes in dog show competitions, such as the prestigious Westminster Kennel Club.[23]

George H. W. Bush, the forty-first president of the United States (1989–1993), played first base for the Yale baseball team in 1948. So a bulldog actually lived in the White House.

At a 1901 University of Georgia football game against an archrival, fans wore badges that read, "Eat 'em, Georgia." Pictured on the badge was a bulldog tearing at a cloth. Some two decades later, Georgia became the Bulldogs, inspired by the breed's dignity and ferocity (ferocious nature). Georgia's bulldog mascot is named Uga (pronounced UG-a). Where does the name come from? *U* for University and *ga* for the abbreviation of Georgia—GA.[24] How tough is the bulldog? Even the United States Marine Corps uses a bulldog as its mascot.

Don't be fooled, though, little dogs can be equally tenacious. The El Paso Chihuahuas (2014–present) of minor-league baseball are nicknamed after the Mexican state of Chihuahua, which borders the city of El Paso, Texas. The Chihuahua is the smallest breed of dog and is named after the Mexican state.

Alternative Team Name: The Georgia Bulldogs are also called the Dawgs.

Other Teams Named Bulldogs: Bowie State University (MD), Mississippi State University, South Carolina State University, Drake University (IA), Fresno State University (CA), Gonzaga University (WA), and University of North Carolina Asheville are among more than forty college athletic teams that go by the nickname Bulldogs.

CHALLENGE #7: ALLITERATIVE NAMES

Alliteration is the repetition of identical letters or sounds in consecutive words. Perhaps it is best experienced in the tongue-twister "Peter Piper picked a peck of pickled peppers." We just learned that the Jacksonville Jaguars are an example of alliteration in a sports team's name. So far in this text we've discussed plenty of teams that use alliteration in their names. How many do you remember? Name at least three. Some of them play in home cities such as San Antonio, Seattle, Edmonton, Los Angeles, and Buffalo.

INSECTS

Salt Lake Bees (2006–present)

You've undoubtedly heard the phrase "Busy as a bee." Well, bees are a symbol of industriousness, especially for people of the Mormon faith, who inhabit the state of Utah in great numbers. Known as the Beehive State, a hive is pictured prominently on the Utah state flag. That's how minor-league baseball's Salt

Lake Bees received their nickname. Over the years, the team has also been called the Salt Lake Stingers (2001–2005) and the Salt Lake Buzz (1994–2000). Their stadium is referred to by fans as the Apiary—a location where beehives are kept. Salt Lake City is the capital of Utah and named for its proximity to the Great Salt Lake—the largest salt water lake in the Western Hemisphere.

Other Teams Named Bees: St Ambrose University (IA) and Savannah College of Art and Design (GA)

Georgia Tech Yellowjackets

There are a swarm of collegiate athletic programs nicknamed the Yellowjackets. These social hunting insects, which are often confused with bees because of their black-and-yellow coloring, are actually wasps and have the ability to sting repeatedly. Perhaps the most prominent school using this nickname is the Georgia Institute of Technology, or Georgia Tech, which has a costumed mascot named Buzz. That's why the Salt Lake Buzz (mentioned above) changed their name; they were sued by Georgia Tech for copyright infringement—using another entity's copyrighted property without permission.[25] *Can't the bees and wasps just get along?* The school actually has a second nickname, the Georgia Tech Ramblin' Wreck, inspired by a 1930 Ford Model A automobile that precedes the football team onto the field.

Did you know that the singer Sting, whose real name is Gordon Sumner, received his nickname from wearing a hoop-striped black-and-yellow sweater onstage?

Other Teams Named Yellowjackets: International American College (MA), Baldwin Wallace University (OH), Graceland University (IA), University of Rochester (NY), and West Virginia State University

The South seems to have the market cornered on insect nicknames. There's the University of Richmond Spiders in Virginia. Georgia's Savannah Sand Gnats, South Carolina's Columbia Fireflies, and North Carolina's Greensboro Grasshoppers are all minor-league baseball teams. But if you go to a Fireflies game, go at night. Why? Parts of their uniforms glow in the dark as a tribute to their namesakes.

There's also the University of South Carolina Sumter Fire Ants. Imagine if they competed against the University of California, Irvine Anteaters. And if the Anteaters win, there could be a bad case of heartburn in the offing.

7

GEOGRAPHY

REGIONAL MONIKERS

University of Tennessee Volunteers

Tennessee is called the Volunteer State for good reason. When it comes to defending their country, the people of Tennessee have always gone far beyond the call of duty. During the fight for Texas in 1846, President James K. Polk needed soldiers for an army to battle Mexican forces. Polk asked each state (at that time, there were only twenty-eight) to contribute twenty-six hundred men. Tennessee had already lost its beloved hero Davy Crockett in the struggle for Texas's independence, but within a week, an amazing thirty thousand Tennesseans reported for militia duty.[1] It is with great respect for the service of the state's citizen soldiers that the University of Tennessee calls its athletic teams the Volunteers.

Davy Crockett was a nineteenth-century American folk hero who was referred to as "King of the Wild Frontier." Crockett died at the Battle of the Alamo in 1836 fighting Mexican forces, where brave US soldiers were badly outnumbered. At the battle's end, several Americans surrendered their arms, only to be brutally executed by their captors. That inspired the rallying cry, "Remember the Alamo!"[2] and spurred many of those volunteers from Tennessee to enlist.

Alternative Team Name: Vols
Another Team Named Volunteers: Logan College (IL)

University of Idaho Vandals

You might think that a team from Idaho would sport the nickname Spuds, Chips, or even Fries. After all, Idaho produces approximately one-third of all the potatoes grown in the United States. So what made the University of Idaho call its teams the Vandals? Well, it's not because they're thieves. At least, not in real life. Back in 1917, the Idaho basketball team played defense with such passion and fervor that a sportswriter reported they "vandalized' the opposing squad. The team was later referred to in print as a gang of "vandals."[3] The new nickname stuck, and a few years later it was officially adopted by the university. Maybe the next time you hear a stadium crowd chant, "De-fense! De-fense!" you'll think "Vandals!"

University of Nebraska Cornhuskers

Many athletic teams—such as the Indiana Hoosiers and the Tennessee Volunteers—bear their state's official nickname. In the state of Nebraska, however, it happened in reverse. The University of Nebraska's sports teams began using the name Cornhuskers first. Eventually, the nickname became so popular that Nebraska decided to officially call itself the Cornhusker State.[4] What is a cornhusker? Ears of corn grow inside of a green, leafy husk. A person or machine that removes the husk from the corn, so that it can be eaten, is called a *cornhusker*. And yes, corn is one of the major crops cultivated in Nebraska. Prior to becoming the Cornhuskers, the University of Nebraska referred to its teams as the Bugeaters, recognizing the insect-devouring bull bats that inhabit the state's open plains. Cornhuskers is certainly the more appetizing choice.

Alternative Team Names: Huskers and Big Red

One Step Prior: Before the husk can be removed, an ear of corn must first be picked from the stalk. To that end, Hoopeston Area High School in Illinois calls its teams the Corn Jerkers, saluting the many laborers who work the fields harvesting corn, one of its state's major crops.

Los Angeles Angels (1961–present)

Baseball's Los Angeles Angels sport a nickname that corresponds perfectly to their city. Los Angeles is called the City of Angels because *los angeles* in Spanish means "the angels." It is the second-largest city by population in the United States (only behind New York City), becoming part of the country as a result of the Mexican-American War (1846–1848). In art and literature, angels are usually associated with bird wings and halos, a circle of light around their heads. The study of angels is known as *angelology*.

© MLB.com

Student: Sorry, I didn't do my homework last night. I was busy with my angelology.

Teacher: Do you mean you were watching an Angels baseball game?

Alternative Team Name: Halos
Another Team Named Angels: Meredith College (NC)

San Diego Padres (1969–present)

The San Diego Padres received their name in a similar fashion to the Angels. *Padre* means "father" or "priest" in Spanish. The nickname honors an historic Roman Catholic mission, San Diego de Alcala, which was founded in the city in the 1700s.[5] The Padres were once owned by Ray Kroc, who was the founder of McDonald's. Gold is part of their team colors, the same as McDonald's golden arches.

The Padres are responsible for a surge in costumed mascots, due to the success of the San Diego Chicken. The Chicken first appeared in 1974. It was played by college student Ted Giannoulas, who appeared at more than five hundred consecutive Padres games, leading the cheers in yellow feathers. The mascot's voiceless antics have been compared to Charlie Chaplin (a physical comedian from the silent film era) in a chicken suit. The original Chicken costume is on display at the National Baseball Hall of Fame and Museum in Cooperstown, New York.

Alternative Team Names: Pods or Friars

New Orleans Pelicans (2013–present)

Pelicans are the state bird of Louisiana, so a perfect nickname for the NBA franchise in New Orleans. These large water birds are recognized by their long beaks and throat pouches, which they use to scoop up small fish swimming near the surface and then drain out the water before swallowing their prey headfirst.[6] Gulls have actually been known to peck at the heads of pelicans to distract them and then steal their fish. Pelicans usually travel in flocks and hunt cooperatively.

Multiples: A group of pelicans is called a *pod.* Whales are also a pod. Several owls are referred to as a parliament. And multiple crows are referred to as a murder. Murder? That poor scarecrow!

New Jersey Devils (1982-present)

© NHL.com

Devils on the frozen ice? The NHL's New Jersey Devils are actually quite at home there. The team is named after the Jersey Devil, a mythical creature that supposedly inhabits the South Jersey Pine Barrens, a heavily wooded area. In early literature, hell wasn't represented as a fiery place. Some of the first literary depictions of hell, such as Dante's *Inferno* in the fourteenth century, describe it as a frozen wasteland. Call that coincidence, because from 1976 to 1982, prior to taking up residence in the Garden State, the Devils franchise played in much colder surroundings as the Colorado Rockies.

In popular culture, the Rolling Stones had a hit song with "Sympathy for the Devil." Charlie Daniels also had success with "The Devil Went Down to Georgia," where the devil, as a musical virtuoso, competes with a boy named Johnny in a fiddle contest, wagering a fiddle made of gold against the boy's soul. The 1958 film *Damn Yankees* was based on Douglass Wallop's 1954 book *The Year the Yankees Lost the Pennant.* The protagonist, a middle-aged baseball fan, sells his soul to a devil-like character for youth and baseball prowess as a member of his beloved but futile Washington Senators in order to defeat the dynastic New York Yankees. *Star Wars: Episode I—The Phantom Menace* (1999) featured the fictional Darth Maul, who wielded a double-sided lightsaber behind a devilish face and protruding horns. And on TV, the cartoonish Powerpuff Girls, Doctor Who, Xena, and even the crew of *Star Trek: The Next Generation* have battled devil-like villains.

Alternative Team Name: Devs
Other Teams Named Devils: Kinki University (Japan) and the University of Sciences in Philadelphia; Duke University is called the Blue Devils; Dickinson

College (PA) is the Red Devils; the men's teams at Mississippi Valley State are nicknamed the Delta Devils, while the women's teams are the Devilettes; and Texas A&M International University goes by the name Dustdevils

CHALLENGE #8: STATE CAPITALS NAMED FOR US PRESIDENTS

The state capital of Nebraska is Lincoln, named after the sixteenth president of the United States, Abraham Lincoln. Three more of the fifty states have capital cities named after US presidents. Can you name that trio of capitals? If you're using a map, most state capitals are designated with the symbol of a star. You can also go online and search both state capitals and US presidents. Then compare the two lists to find the correct answers. (Just so you know, Washington, DC, is not a state capital.)

SPORTS TOPOGRAPHY

Colorado Rockies (1993–present)

Colorado's pro baseball team is nicknamed the Rockies, recognizing the snow-capped mountain range that dominates the state's landscape. Millions of years ago, shifting continental plates created periods of building and transformed the level plains into the Rocky Mountains, which were shaped by water and ice after they rose from ancient oceans. The immense mountain range stretches for more than three thousand miles—from British Columbia in western Canada to New Mexico in the southwestern United States.[7]

The Rockies play at Coors Field in the city of Denver. During the stadium's construction, workers uncovered a number of dinosaur fossils, including a seven-foot triceratops skull. That discovery led the Rockies to choose a triceratops mascot named Dinger—baseball slang for a home run, which happens quite often considering the elevation of Coors Field is a mile above sea level, providing less air friction on a batted baseball.

Alternative Team Name: Rox
Other Teams Named Rockies: Colorado Rockies (1976–1982) of the NHL

Colorado Avalanche (1995-present)

Mountains at high altitudes (the Rockies are more than fourteen thousand feet high) mean lots of snow. Accordingly, Colorado's professional hockey team is called the Avalanche. But don't worry—their fans can cheer all they want. It's a myth that avalanches are caused by people's voices. They really occur when plates of dry snow fracture, breaking apart as they slide (sometimes beneath the weight of someone hiking or climbing). Within five seconds of being triggered, avalanches can reach speeds of between 60–80 MPH. Why are they so dangerous? A mountain avalanche can release as much as three hundred thousand cubic yards of fast-moving snow.[8] That's the equivalent of twenty football fields filled ten yards deep with the icy stuff, generating enormous destructive power.

Alternative Team Name: Avs

South Park Elementary Cows

Colorado is also the home of the animated TV series *South Park*. That's where characters Stan Marsh, Kyle Broflovski, Eric Cartman, and Kenny McCormick attend South Park Elementary between their outlandish and comical adventures. The school's sports teams certainly have a nickname. Do you know it? Bovines would be a good clue. Well, it's the South Park Elementary Cows, named after the black-and-white Holstein cows that dot the show's mountainous countryside.

Portland Trailblazers (1970-present)

The Portland Trailblazers of the NBA are named in honor of wilderness explorers, like those of the Lewis and Clark expedition (1803–1806), who blazed a trail through the thickly wooded northwestern wilderness for settlers to eventually follow. From where does the word *trailblazer* come? Well, a trail is something to follow along, like a path through the forest. Now, how about the blaze part? Horses have blazes on their faces. It's a group of white hairs clustered together, creating a long vertical patch or mark. Copying this, explorers would take their hatchets and cut a white blaze into a tree trunk by removing its brown bark. These tree blazes would mark the trail. Hence, we have the word *trailblazer*.

Alternative Team Name: Blazers

Other Teams Named Trailblazers: Atlanta Metropolitan College (GA) and Dixie State University (UT); the University of Alabama at Birmingham is called the Blazers.

Fun Fact: Football games normally begin with a coin flip. But did you know that the city of Portland, Oregon, received its name through the flip of a coin in 1845? Each of its two founders wanted to name it after his hometown.[9] One founder was from Portland, Maine. The other was from Boston, Massachusetts. Now guess who won that coin flip? The 1835 copper penny that was flipped is known as the Portland Penny.

San Jose Earthquakes (1974-1988, 1994-1999, 2005-present)

Major League Soccer's team in San Jose was nicknamed—with initial criticism from the media—the Earthquakes because the city is located close to the San Andreas Fault. The fault line extends more than eight hundred miles through the state, posing a high degree of earthquake risk along its three segments—the northern, central, and southern. Earthquakes are caused by a sudden release of energy in the earth's crust, creating seismic (energy) waves.[10] An earthquake interrupted baseball's 1989 World Series between a pair of California teams—the Oakland Athletics and San Francisco Giants—when it struck the Bay Area on October 17, causing substantial damage to both cities and delaying the series by more than a week.

Alternative Team Names: Quakes and Goonies (Why the Goonies? After several consecutive late comeback victories, an Earthquakes player told the

Bad Idea: Obviously, the press disliked the nickname Earthquakes because those events are destructive and life-threatening matters. Still, the name seemed to resonate with fans. When the ABA's Memphis Sounds moved to Baltimore, Maryland, in 1975, the franchise decided to rename itself. The owners inexplicably chose to call their team the Baltimore Hustlers. This time, both the press and league officials put a stop to it before the Hustlers ever took the basketball court. The new nickname? The Baltimore Claws. The franchise folded, however, after playing only three exhibition games that season, all of which were defeats.

The men's baseball team at California State University, Long Beach is called the Dirtbags. This nickname is not shared by any of the university's other teams.

press, "Goonies never say die!" It was a reference from the 1985 film *The Goonies*. And that soon became the team's motto.)

Another Team Named Earthquakes: A minor-league baseball team in Rancho Cucamonga, California, calls itself the Quakes.

University of Hawaii at Hilo Vulcans

The University of Hawaii at Hilo uses the nickname Vulcans for its sports teams. No, the students are not all big fans of Mr. Spock from the TV and movie series *Star Trek*, who is from the fictional planet Vulcan, which was also the name of the Roman god of fire. It seems the Hawaiian Islands (there are eight major islands) were formed by volcanic activity and undersea magma called the Hawaii hotspot. Correspondingly, Hawaii is home to a number of volcanoes, including the earth's most massive, Mauna Loa, as well as one of its most active, Kilauea, which is between three hundred thousand and six hundred thousand years old. During the spring of 2018, Kilauea had an explosive eruption, spewing firebombs of molten lava and reshaping the surrounding landscape.

CITYSCAPES

Minnesota Twins (1961–present)

© MLB.com

MLB's Minnesota Twins are named after the twin cities of Minneapolis and St. Paul. Twin cities are closely located geographically and usually grow into each other over time. They sometimes become seen as one, often making the border that separates them meaningless. Other examples of twin cities in the United States are Dallas and Fort Worth in Texas and Akron and Canton in Ohio. The European city of Budapest in Hungary actually began as the twin cities of Buda and Pest before they joined into one.

Alternative Team Name: Twinkies (slang for people who live in twin cities; can also refer to real twins)

Another Team Named Twins: Columbia-Greene Community College (NY)

New York Mets (1962-present)

The New York Mets are really named the Metropolitans. A metropolitan area or region is one that is densely populated. That perfectly describes New York City, the nation's largest, where some 8 million people live. In fact, one of New York City's five boroughs—Brooklyn—would be the fourth most populous city in the United States on its own. People living in a metropolitan area are said to have culture and sophistication. Fittingly, New York City has many museums, art galleries, and theaters. In the comics, Superman/Clark Kent lives in such a large city, called Metropolis.

© MLB.com

Alternative Team Names: The Amazin's and Miracle Mets (for winning the 1969 World Series against astronomical odds)

Arsenal Gunners (1886-present)

The Arsenal Football Club is a professional soccer team based in London, England. The club was formed in the late nineteenth century by workers at the Royal Arsenal in the Borough of Woolwich, southeast London. An *arsenal* is a collection of weapons and military equipment stored together. The Arsenal F.C. is nicknamed the Gunners, sporting a trio of cannons on their crest (or team badge), because of the long military history surrounding the area, including the Royal Arsenal, Royal Artillery Regiment, and various military hospitals.[11]

Pittsburgh Penguins (1967-present)

The NHL's Pittsburgh Penguins received their nickname through a name-the-team contest. More than seven hundred people in Pittsburgh submitted the name Penguins. Why? Was it the pleasing alliteration of the double *P*, also found in the Pittsburgh Pirates? More likely it was because the arena in which the fledgling franchise was scheduled to play, the Pittsburgh Civic Arena, was already known as the Igloo.[12] That made a perfect cold-weather connection. But don't some penguins live in the desert? You might know that Antarctica is technically a desert, but this isn't a trick. The Galapagos penguin actually lives near the equator, off the mainland of Ecuador, while the jackass penguin, named for its donkey-like braying call, inhabits the continent of Africa.

Alternative Team Name: Pens

Other Teams Named Penguins: Clark College (WA), Youngstown State University (OH), and Dominican University of California

REACHING THE HEIGHTS

West Virginia University Mountaineers

West Virginia is nicknamed the Mountain State. So it's quite appropriate that the University of West Virginia calls its athletic teams the Mountaineers. A mountaineer is a person who lives in a mountainous area. That would definitely be West Virginia. The state is home to thirty-seven individual mountains. Many of those mountains are part of the Appalachian Range, which stretches approximately fifteen hundred miles from Canada to Alabama.[13] These mountains were formed roughly 480 million years ago when portions of the earth's crust moved. The state's motto is *Mountani Semper Liberi,* meaning "Mountaineers Are Always Free."

Other Teams Named Mountaineers: Appalachian State University (NC), Berea College (KY), Eastern Oklahoma State University, Mansfield University (PA), and Southern Vermont College

Fun Fact: What's the difference between a mountain and a hill? Well, a mountain is steeper than a hill and usually has a peak, or highest point. Different countries use varying minimum heights to qualify mountains (from two thousand to eight thousand feet). So there is no universally accepted standard. Still, some mountains dwarf those standards. Mount Everest, the highest mountain on earth, located in the Himalayas of Asia, stands 29,035 feet above sea level. You can go online to find the highest known mountain in our solar system. Hint: It resides on the fourth planet from our sun.

Atlanta Falcons (1966–present)

The NFL's Atlanta Falcons received their nickname when a schoolteacher from Georgia submitted it in a naming contest. "The falcon is proud and dignified, with great courage and fight. It never drops its prey. It is deadly and has a great sporting tradition," was the teacher's reasoning behind the suggestion.[14] Falcons are a species of raptor. An adult falcon's long, tapered wings enable it

© iStock/FRANKHILDEBRAND

to fly at high speeds and change directions quickly. In fact, the peregrine falcon has been recorded diving from steep altitudes at speeds of more than 200 MPH. That makes it the fastest-moving animal on earth.

The sporting tradition with this bird of prey is called *falconry*, which dates back to about 2000 BCE. A person called a *falconer* trains his or her falcon to hunt, mostly smaller birds, on command. There are currently numerous falconry clubs in North America and Great Britain.

Alternative Team Nicknames: Dirty Birds, Grits Blitz (defense)
Other Teams Named Falcons: US Air Force Academy (CO), Bowling Green University (OH), Daytona State University (FL), Fairmont State University (WV), Seattle Pacific University (WA), and University of Wisconsin–River Falls

Denver Nuggets (1976–present)

Denver, the capital of Colorado, is called the Mile-High City. That's because Denver's official elevation (5,280 feet) is one mile above sea level. The name of the NBA's Denver Nuggets comes from the Colorado mining boom of the nineteenth century, when people rushed to the area hoping to make their fortune by panning for gold and silver nuggets. Panning is one of the simplest ways to find gold, and you can do it yourself: Take the dirt and sand from the bed of a mountain stream and place it in a special mining pan filled with water. Gently shake the pan, separating the water from the sediment. Any gold, which is heavier than the dirt or sand, will sink to the bottom.[15] You can go online to find expert video tutorials on how to properly pan for gold. Panning for gold makes you a prospector—one who explores an area looking for mineral deposits or oil.

8

INDUSTRIAL REVOLUTION

TEAMS OF INDUSTRY

Pittsburgh Steelers (1933–present)

© NFL.com

Several sports teams receive their names from the industries that dominate their region. Pittsburgh earned the name Steel City because of the vast amount of steel produced there. So it's not surprising that the city's football team is nicknamed the Steelers. The team even sports the steel industry logo, which was once placed on all US Steel products, upon their helmets. The logo's three diamond-like shapes represent the elements needed to produce steel: coal, iron ore, and steel scrap. Steel has been produced for thousands of years using different methods. Modern production methods have made steel one of the most common materials in the world; 1.3 billion tons are produced annually.[1] It is a major component in the production of buildings, infrastructure (roads and bridges), tools, ships, and cars.

The Steelers are the only pro football team with their logo on just one side of their helmets. It's been that way since 1962, when ownership instructed the team's equipment manager to place the new logo on the right side of the helmets, to see how it would look. Fans connected to the logo on just one side, and the next year, the Steelers switched from gold-colored to black helmets so it would stand out even more.[2]

Alternative Team Names: Steel Curtain (defense) and Black and Gold

Cleveland Molly Maguires (1912–1914)

Prior to becoming the Indians, Cleveland's pro baseball franchise was nicknamed the Molly Maguires. The name springs from a secret group of coal miners, originally begun in Ireland, who battled against their bosses for better working conditions and the formation of a union. These fights often became violent on both sides. In fact, in the late nineteenth century, twenty members of the Molly Maguires were sentenced to death after being convicted in Pennsylvania of serious crimes, including murder. Ten were actually executed. Many others, however, were eventually pardoned.[3] Today most historians agree that the legal system was unfairly stacked against them due to the political influence of their wealthy and powerful coal bosses.

Chicago Bulls (1966–present)

© NBA.com

Chicago's NBA team is nicknamed the Bulls. At the beginning of the twentieth century, Chicago became famous for its stockyards and was home to the country's biggest meat-packers. It was the city from which hogs, cattle, and sheep found their way to the nation's dinner tables. In his poem entitled "Chicago," poet Carl Sandburg (1878–1967) even referred to Chicago as "hog butcher for the world":

> Hog Butcher for the World,
> Tool Maker, Stacker of Wheat,
> Player with Railroads and the Nation's Freight Handler;
> Stormy, husky, brawling,
> City of the Big Shoulders:

Famed basketball player Michael Jordan led the Chicago Bulls to six World Championships within a decade, doing so in a pair of three-peats (three in a row) from 1991 to 1993 and 1996 to 1998. From 1993 to 1994, Jordan left basketball to pursue a career in baseball, playing in the minor leagues with the Chicago White Sox organization.

Other Teams Named Bulls: University of South Florida and State University of New York at Buffalo

Owning It: The word *three-peat* was coined, or first used, by Los Angeles Lakers player Byron Scott. He did so after the Lakers won their second straight NBA championship in 1988. They lost the following year in the NBA Finals, unable to attain their goal of three successive titles. However, Scott's coach at the time, Pat Riley, went out and trademarked the newly minted phrase. So Riley now owns the word that Scott invented. I suppose that could cause some friction between a player and a coach.

Green Bay Packers (1919-present)

What's a packer? In 1919, football's fledgling Green Bay Packers received their name from the Indian Packing Company, who sponsored the team by buying their equipment and allowing them to practice on the company athletic field.[4] Green Bay is situated in the state of Wisconsin, which is known for its production of cheese. Hence, Packers fans are often called Cheeseheads. Yes, that's a compliment. The Packers are also the only community-owned franchise in a major American sports league. This means no single individual or corporation owns the team; instead, the Packers are owned by more than 350,000 stockholders, with no one being allowed to own more than approximately 4 percent of the team.

Alternative Team Name: The Pack

Milwaukee Brewers (1970-present)

MLB's Milwaukee Brewers owe their name to the city's brewing industry. Milwaukee is known as the beer capital of the world, and many brewing companies call the city home. The Brewers mascot, Bernie Brewer, used to celebrate hometown heroics by going down a slide into a huge mug of beer. His actions undoubtedly gave new meaning to the concept of hitting a staggering home run! The practice was eventually changed—the slide remained but the mug was removed—after complaints that it encouraged excessive drinking and rowdiness at the ballpark.

Alternative Team Name: The Brew Crew
Other Teams Named Brewers: Vassar College (NY)

Columbus Blue Jackets (2000-present)

During the American Civil War, many of the blue coats worn by the northern Union Army were manufactured in the city of Columbus, Ohio. That led this hockey franchise to adopt the name Blue Jackets. Ohio contributed more of its populace to the Union Army than any other state. The state of Ohio produced a number of famed Civil War figures, including General Ulysses S. Grant, who would later become the eighteenth president of the United States and appear on the $50 bill. The city of Columbus was also host to several large military bases at that time.[5]

Alternative Team Name: Jackets

University of Florida Gators and New York Red Bulls (2006-present)

The sports drink Gatorade owes its name to the University of Florida Gators. The replenishing powers of the mixture were first tested and refined with help from the university's athletic teams, which often had to practice in the sweltering heat and humidity of a Florida summer. The company that makes the energy drink Red Bull owns a MLS team called the New York Red Bulls. How embarrassing would it be for their players to tire out on the field? By the way, a soccer field is often referred to as the *pitch.*

CHALLENGE #9: CHANGING MILLIONS INTO BILLIONS

Earlier in this chapter, we learned that 1.3 billion tons of steel are produced annually, or every year. But exactly what would that look like written out numerically? And how do we tell the difference between thousands, millions, and billions?

Well, the thousands occupy the fourth, fifth, and sixth number columns:

one thousand = 1,000; fifty thousand = 50,000;
two hundred thousand = 200,000

Millions occupy the seventh, eighth, and ninth columns:

one million = 1,000,000; fifty million = 50,000,000;
two hundred million = 200,000,000

Billions occupy the three columns after that—the tenth, eleventh, and twelfth:

one billion = 1,000,000,000; fifty billion = 50,000,000,000;
two hundred billion = 200,000,000,000

Here is 1.3 million written out numerically: 1,300,000. Now you turn it into 1.3 billion, the number of tons of steel produced annually.

THE NEED FOR SPEED

Detroit Pistons (1941–present)

Basketball's Pistons franchise started out as the Fort Wayne Pistons, playing in Indiana. Zollner, the corporation that owned them, had a foundry that made engine pistons for cars, boats, and locomotives.[6] In 1957, however, the team moved to Detroit, Michigan, and the nickname Pistons was perfect, because Detroit is known as the Motor City. It's where Henry Ford started mass-producing cars. Ford developed the assembly line, a process in which each worker in a line performs a single task, such as securing the headlights, as the cars roll past to their completion. This allowed cars to be manufactured at a much faster rate. Detroit's NBA team is appropriately called the Pistons. A piston is a fast-moving part of a car's engine that helps create power. Three of the biggest car manufactures in Detroit are General Motors, the Ford Motor Company, and Chrysler.

Alternative Team Name: Bad Boys (referring to their championship squads of 1989 and 1990, which were noted for their overly aggressive and physical style of play)

Seattle Supersonics (1967–2008)

Like Detroit, the city of Seattle, Washington, is connected to an industry: building jet aircraft. Among the major companies that assemble planes there is Boeing, which created the 747. Fittingly, Seattle's former NBA team was called the Supersonics. Jet aircraft that break the sound barrier by flying faster than 768 MPH (the speed of sound) are said to be traveling at a supersonic speed. But aircraft aren't the only things that are supersonic. The tip of a bullwhip can break the sound barrier (its crack is actually a small sonic boom), as can bullets leaving a gun.

Alternative Team Name: Sonics

Houston Rockets (1971–present)

Rockets can also travel at supersonic speeds. This basketball franchise started out in California as the San Diego Rockets. The nickname Rockets was chosen because San Diego was a fast-growing city that was on the move. When the team relocated to Houston in 1971, however, the name became instantly associated with the National Aeronautics and Space Administration (NASA) and the space program, which is based in that Texas city. A rocket is a missile or vehicle that obtains thrust from an engine that works by action and reaction, pushing a rocket forward. The first rockets were designed by the Chinese in the thirteenth century and were called *fire arrows*.[7]

© NBA.com

Early sci-fi writers such as H. G. Wells (*The War of the Worlds*) and Jules Verne (*Journey to the Center of the Earth* and *Twenty Thousand Leagues under the Sea*) wrote stories of how rockets would one day fuel interplanetary travel. Those stories inspired many future scientists, including Dr. Robert Goddard, the father of modern rocketry. In the animated film *Jimmy Neutron: Boy Genius* (2001), science-loving protagonist Jimmy Neutron builds himself a robotic dog named Goddard.

Murray State University Racers

The athletic teams at Murray State University used to be called the Thoroughbreds—a significant nickname for a state that hosts the Kentucky Derby, contested on the first Saturday in May each year for three-year-old Thoroughbreds.

© iStock/JulieJJ

Newspaper headline writers, however, didn't appreciate how much space the word Thoroughbreds took up, so the name started to become shortened in print. The press knocked it down to T-Breds, 'Breds, Horse Racers, and then finally Racers, which stuck with the school back in the 1950s.[8]

Faster Horses: The Kentucky Derby is often called "the most exciting two minutes in sports." That's about how long it takes a Thoroughbred, which can run at approximately 40 MPH, to race its 1¼-mile distance. Pretty fast for a fifteen-hundred-pound animal.

Indiana Pacers (1967–present)

The NBA's Indiana Pacers represent, in part, a different kind of horsepower. The state of Indiana is known for its harness-racing pacers (Standardbred horses). Standardbreds usually race a distance of one mile. Instead of a jockey on their backs, pacers are directed by a driver who is pulled behind them in a small carriage called a *sulky*. The name also refers to the pace car in Indiana's most famous sporting event—the Indianapolis 500. That race is a five-hundred-mile event held annually on the Sunday of Memorial Day weekend at the Indianapolis Motor Speedway. The pace car leads the competing cars onto the track, limiting the speed of the racers, who must follow behind it. The pace car also comes onto the track during periods of caution, such as when a wreck or other obstruction creates a dangerous situation. That's called racing under a yellow flag.

Other Teams Named Pacers: Marywood University (PA), University of South Carolina Aiken, and William Peace University (NC)

Indianapolis Colts (1984–present)

The NFL's Indianapolis Colts actually started out in the state of Maryland, as the Baltimore Colts (1953–1983). The team received that nickname because of the state's strong affiliation with the racing and breeding of Thoroughbred horses. In fact, the Preakness Stakes is held in Baltimore on the third Saturday of May each year. It is the second jewel of Thoroughbred racing's Triple Crown. The other two jewels are the Kentucky Derby and the Belmont Stakes (held in New York). Some of history's fastest racehorses, such as Secretariat, Seattle Slew, American Pharoah, and Justify have won the Triple Crown. When the Colts made the move to Indianapolis in 1984, they decided to keep their name, which also reflects Indiana's own heritage with horses.

© iStock/ilbusca

Los Angeles Clippers (1978–present)

Clippers are fast sailing ships. They had their greatest impact in the United States during the California Gold Rush of 1849. These wind-powered ships with multiple sails made the trip between New York City and San Francisco by going around the far tip of South America, known as Cape Horn. It routinely took more than one hundred days to complete the 13,225-mile voyage. That trek eventually became 5,000 miles shorter with the opening of the Panama Canal in 1914, providing a passageway between the Atlantic and Pacific Oceans and cutting the sea trip down to about one month.[9] The NBA's Los Angeles

Taking It Slow: Apparently some teams have no desire to sport a speedy nickname. The University of Maryland Terrapins are among them. A terrapin is actually a turtle. We can only hope that Maryland's track team is well acquainted with Aesop's story of "The Tortoise and the Hare." The University of Santa Cruz Banana Slugs also fall into this category. Found in the northwestern forests of North America, these large yellow slugs with black spots move very slowly on only one muscular foot. In case you didn't know, slugs resemble snails without the shell.

Clippers, who called the coastal city of San Diego home from 1978 to 1984, owe their nickname to these fleet sailing vessels.

Alternative Team Name: Clips
Other Teams Named Clippers: Concordia College (NY) and University of Maine at Machias

CHALLENGE #10: HOW MANY LAPS TO A MILE?

Earlier in this chapter, we learned that the Indianapolis 500, which is held at the Indianapolis Motor Speedway, is a 500-mile car race. That's a lot of left-hand turns around an oval track. Ever wonder how many laps it would take to make 500 miles? Well, let's figure it out. We already have the distance: 500 miles. Now we need to know the size of the track. That happens to be 2.5 miles. To get the answer, we need to divide the distance by the size of the track (500 divided by 2.5). The outcome of that equation would give us the exact number of laps it would take. Mathletes, start your engines!

FOREIGN STUDIES

OH, CANADA!

Montreal Canadiens (1917–present)

Hockey is the national winter sport of Canada. (It's lacrosse in the summer.) The word *hockey* may have possibly come from *hoquet*, a French word for a shepherd's curved or hooked staff. How far in time does the game go back in some form or another? In Egypt, four-thousand-year-old carvings have been found of teams competing with sticks and slapping at projectile objects.[1] Of course, most people today envision hockey being played on an ice rink or frozen pond, with participants wearing ice skates. Because of the sport's connection to Canada, it's no wonder one of the original franchises in the NHL is the Montreal Canadiens. The club's official name, however, is *le Club de hockey Canadien*.

Alternative Team Name: Habs (an abbreviation for *Les Habitants*, a name for early French settlers in Canada in the 1600s)[2]

Toronto Maple Leafs (1927–present)

A maple leaf is the centerpiece of the Canadian flag. It is one of the most prominent symbols in Canada and signifies the country's respect for nature—including the maple tree, which is used to produce maple syrup and wood products. Fittingly, the hockey team in Toronto—Canada's largest city, with a population of

© NHL.com

more than 2.5 million—is nicknamed the Maple Leafs. Previously the team was called the St. Patricks, hoping to attract the support of Toronto's Irish population. But in 1927 the team's new owner, Conn Smythe, who had served with Canada's Maple Leaf regiment during World War I, renamed the franchise.[3]

Alternative Team Name: Leafs

Edmonton Oilers (1973–present)

The production of petroleum is a major industry in Canada, which is among the largest oil-producing countries in the world. There are believed to be more oil reserves still untapped in Canada than in the rest of the world combined. The province of Alberta produces more oil than any other region of the country, and the city of Edmonton is Alberta's capital. An overwhelming percentage of Edmonton's economy stems from the petroleum industry.[4] Hence, its hockey team is named the Oilers. Legendary hockey player Wayne Gretzky, who is nicknamed "The Great One," won four Stanley Cups playing with Edmonton.

Other Teams Named Oilers: Houston Oilers (NFL; 1960–1996) and University of Findlay (OH)

Toronto Raptors (1995–present)

The NBA team in Toronto goes by the nickname Raptors. A raptor is a fast-running predator— a birdlike carnivorous (meat-eating) dinosaur. That's an appropriate name for a team from Canada, which is well known for its dinosaur fossils. Dinosaur Provincial Park in Alberta is one of the  world's richest locations to find such fossils. More than five hundred specimens have been dug up or unearthed at the park.[5] Perhaps the 1993 film *Jurassic Park* is most responsible for popularizing the image of the raptor.

© NBA.com

Another Team Named Raptors: Bard College (NY)

Calgary Stampeders (1935–present)

The CFL's Calgary Stampeders receive their nickname from the annual rodeo and festival held every July in Calgary, Alberta. The Calgary Stampede, a ten-day event, routinely draws an attendance of more than 1 million people. Parades and rodeo events such as bull riding, barrel racing, and bareback riding are among the highlights. Local residents dress in cowboy attire and host pancake breakfasts, inviting visitors to join them. The largest of these pancake breakfasts feeds up to sixty thousand people. Now that's hospitality!

Alternative Team Names: Stamps and Horsemen

Vancouver Canucks (1970–present)

The character of Johnny Canuck first appeared in a Canadian political cartoon in 1869. However, it was during World War II that the character was reinvented as a comic book hero who battled real-life villains such as Adolf Hitler, in much the same way as Steve Rodgers, aka Captain America, battled Nazis in US comics. The term *Canuck* is also slang for a Canadian.[6] So the NHL's Vancouver Canucks actually mirror baseball's New York Yankees in that regard.

CHALLENGE #11: USING COMIC BOOK HEROES IN SPORTS

Johnny Canuck was a Canadian comic book hero who eventually inspired the name of a professional sports franchise—the Vancouver Canucks. Make a list of your favorite heroes from the comics, TV, or movies. Then answer these questions: At which sports would each of your heroes particularly excel? Explain how any superpowers they possess might give them a distinct advantage against their opponents. Would it be a fair contest? If not, how might you change the rules of a given sport to make it more competitive whenever one of your heroes enters the game?

DOWN UNDER

Matildas (1995–present)

The Australian national women's soccer team is named the Matildas. The name is inspired by their country's famed bush ballad "Waltzing Matilda," which is also considered to be the unofficial national anthem of Australia. The ballad is filled with slang. A *matilda* is a swag, or bag, used to carry one's belongings, including probably a rollup bed. The traveler in the song, an itinerant worker, is on foot, walking or waltzing through the countryside. Being hungry, he catches a stray sheep to eat. When the sheep's owner and the authorities confront him, the traveler is unwilling to be caught (and most likely beaten or arrested), and instead drowns himself in a billabong, or watering hole. His ghost then haunts the area. It is a song that, at its core, speaks out against hardship and the oppression of the underprivileged.[7]

Prior to becoming the Matildas, Australia's national women's squad was called the Female Socceroos, combining the words *soccer* and *kangaroo*.

Adelaide Bite (2010-present)

The Adelaide Bite are a pro baseball team in Australia. Their name comes from the Great Australian Bight, a large open bay off parts of the southern coast of Australia, punctuated by the faces of high cliffs, rock platforms, and surfing beaches.[8] A *bight* is a curve or recess in a coastline. The Great Australian Bight is inhabited by the great white shark, which the team, the Bite—spelled differently to suggest a shark bite—features on its logo.

The nicknames of other Australian sports teams also highlight their continent's rather unique wildlife. Pro rugby teams have used the nicknames Kangaroos and Wallabies since the late nineteenth century. Their female counterparts are the Jillaroos and Wallaroos. The teams for adolescents are ideally

© iStock/4FR

called Joeys, which are infant marsupials (mammals with pouches to carry their young). These marsupials include koalas, opossums, Tasmanian devils, wombats, and, of course, kangaroos and wallabies.

Brisbane Bandits (2010–present)

Baseball's Brisbane Bandits brings to mind that Great Britain used Australia as a penal colony, starting in the late eighteenth century. Prisoners were sent to Australia to be exiled after 1776, when the American Colonies gained their independence and the British could no longer send prisoners there.

LAND OF THE RISING SUN

Japanese Baseball

Japan was given the name Land of the Rising Sun by ancient Chinese imperials because of its position east (where the sun rises) of China.[9] Baseball is considered to be Japan's national pastime, and the country has adopted the names of some of the most famous US teams. For example, the Yomiuri Giants sport the same team colors and basic uniform design of our San Francisco Giants, which were once the New York Giants before relocating to the West Coast. Japanese baseball also boasts teams named Tigers, Lions, and Eagles. Of course, Japan is an island nation, surrounded on all sides by the Pacific Ocean. Hence, many of

© iStock/traffic_analyzer

their nicknames are inspired by the sea—Whales, BayStars, BlueWave, Pearls, Marines, and Carp (a type of fish).

Chunichi Dragons (1950–present)

In Asian culture, the dragon is a symbol of power, strength, and good luck for deserving people. Also, anyone who becomes outstanding in their chosen field of work—music, martial arts, painting, teaching, farming, etc.—is considered to be a dragon. Aspiring to that highest-level of skill, Japanese baseball sports a team named the Chunichi Dragons.

Other Teams Named Dragons: Sichuan Dragons (Chinese baseball), Drexel University, Minnesota State Moorhead, Tiffin University (OH), and Paris Junior College (TX)

Punctuation Solution: One Japanese team is called the Nippon-Ham Fighters. Take note of the hyphen (-) between Nippon and Ham, which is a major Japanese food processing company. The hyphen in the name is fairly new. That's because foreigners had great confusion about the team's name without it. Some believed the team was called the Ham Fighters, who either fought against ham or fought using ham as a meaty weapon. Now, with the hyphen in place, it's clear to see that Nippon and Ham are merged, and the team is named simply the Fighters.

CHALLENGE #12: PUNCTUATION AND MEANING

A hyphen is used to join words together, indicating that they have a combined meaning. The use of such punctuation can dramatically change meaning (as seen with the Fighters baseball team above).

Here's a punctuation challenge: Add a hyphen in the correct place to make *man* fearful instead of the *tiger*.

Careful, man eating tiger.

Add a hyphen to the sentence below to work a total of twenty-four hours in a row.

You will be needed to work twenty four hour shifts.

Now, add a hyphen to the sentence below to work a total of eighty hours.

You will be needed to work twenty four hour shifts.

SECOND OFFICIAL TIMEOUT: CREATING A TEAM TO PLAY IN WICHITA, KANSAS

Okay, here's our second official timeout.

During our first timeout, you were given a chance to create a new sports team for an area with which you're well acquainted—your home city or state. This time around, you'll create a team for another city that currently doesn't have a major professional sports franchise. Not to worry, though. We'll give you the needed background on the area. Your job is to use that local history to create an appropriate name for a brand new sports team. Here we go . . .

Wichita, Kansas: Wichita is the largest city in the state of Kansas. It has a population of close to four hundred thousand and is situated on the banks of the Arkansas River. Back in the 1860s, the city began as a trading post along a route called the Chisolm Trail, where ranchers would take their livestock on cattle drives toward Kansas railroad stations to be shipped east. That earned Wichita the nickname Cowtown. In the 1920s and 1930s, several aircraft companies built their planes in Wichita and it became known as the Air Capital of the World. Continuing the theme of flight, the city's largest newspaper is called the *Wichita Eagle.* Wichita can also experience extreme weather during the spring and summer months, including hailstorms, thunderstorms, and tornadoes. For those of you who are fans of fast food, Pizza Hut was founded in Wichita by a pair of college students.[10]

Now, let's brainstorms some ideas together. Baseballs can fly out of a stadium for home runs. That could link nicely with Wichita's aviation connection. Key words like *jets, runways,* and *pilots* might help us to create a team name. In basketball, dunks can be thunderous, like Wichita's summer weather. Football teams can advance down the field, just like the fast-moving trains that once transported cattle east from Wichita. And pizza with tomato sauce, cheese, and various toppings? Well, that's just yummy and very inspiring.

All right—you take it from here. Grab a sheet of paper and try this challenge: Create three possible names for teams in Wichita, Kansas: a baseball team, a basketball team, and a football team. Beside each name, give a reason why it is a good name both for a team from Wichita and for that particular sport. Perhaps you'd like to choose a different sport. Make sure to explain why your nickname might fit that other sport so well.

10

PEOPLE AND POLITICS

MIDWEST LANGUAGE FEST

Indiana Hoosiers

Most states use some variant of their name to describe their residents. For example, people who live in New York are called New Yorkers. People from Florida are called Floridians. However, residents of Indiana are called Hoosiers. Why? Well, folk legend has it that during the early frontier days of the region, visitors approaching a cabin in the woods worried about being shot as unfriendly trespassers. So they would call to the cabin, announcing themselves. The inhabitants of the cabin would shout back, "Who's there?" But their Appalachian twang would make it sound more like, "Who'sh'ere?" Eventually, that response became *Hoosier*.[1] The state widely adopted that name and Indiana University Bloomington chose it as the name for the school's sports teams.

Check out the 1986 movie *Hoosiers*. It's about a small-town Indiana high school basketball team and their coach with a troubled past competing for the state championship. It is widely regarded as one of the best sports films ever made.

Other Representative Team Names: Montreal Canadiens of hockey, Miami Floridians (1968–1972) of pro basketball, the NFL's Houston Texans, and the Utes of the University of Utah; Pittsburgh Americans (1936–1937) of pro football, New York Americans (1931–1956) of pro soccer, and New York Americans (1925–1942) of pro hockey (all also known colloquially as the Amerks). Currently, hockey's Rochester Americans are referred to as the Amerks.

Cleveland Cavaliers (1970–present)

In the summer of 2014, NBA basketball player
LeBron James, who was born in Akron, Ohio,
left the Miami Heat to rejoin the Cleveland
Cavaliers, where he had started his professional
career straight out of high school. Two years

© NBA.com

later, Cleveland (aka Believeland) won their first NBA Championship. The
word *cavalier* is quite interesting. It first appeared in 1659 and was used to describe Royalist supporters of Kings Charles I and II during and after the English
Civil War. Later on, the word came to describe a particular type of frivolous at-
titude possessed by men who cared more about their own vanity (their position
in society and appearance) than about national problems.[2] But the NBA team
undoubtedly chose the name for its third meaning: a gentleman trained in arms
(weapons) and horsemanship, such as a valiant knight.

Alternative Team Name: Cavs
Other Teams Named Cavaliers: University of Virginia and Concordia University (OR)

Kansas City Royals (1969–present)

The Kansas City Royals baseball team owes its nickname to the American Royal
livestock show and rodeo held annually in Kansas City, Missouri, since 1899.
Livestock is a huge part of Missouri's economy.[3] Interestingly, baseball mitts are
often made from cowhide.

Alternative Team Name: Blue Crew
Other Teams Named Royals: Pro basketball's Cincinnati Royals (1957–1972),
Utah Royals of women's soccer, and the Montreal Royals of minor-league
baseball (1896–1960) and international rugby (1939)

Self-evident: Outside the United States, *football* means the sport Americans
know as soccer. Ask most sports fans in the United States, though, how
many players per team are on a soccer field and there could be hesitation in
an answer. In hopes of curing that, the United States boasts the United Soccer League's Indy Eleven, which calls Indianapolis home. Remember this
team's name and you'll know exactly how many players are on the pitch.

Lincoln Memorial University Railsplitters

© LincolnMemorialRailspliters.com

This Tennessee university is home to the Abraham Lincoln Library and Museum. Lincoln was often portrayed as a railsplitter—someone who splits logs with an ax to make a wooden rail fence. During his 1860 presidential campaign, Lincoln, who stood six-foot-four (even without his stovepipe hat), was known as the "Rail Candidate."

Lincoln is quoted as saying, "Give me six hours to chop down a tree and I will spend the first four sharpening the ax."[4]

Watersmeet Nimrods

© WatersmeetHC.com

The names of high school teams rarely make an impact outside of their immediate locales. But in 2003 the cable sports network ESPN defied that logic by featuring the Watersmeet Nimrods in a national ad campaign. Located on Michigan's Upper Peninsula, Watersmeet High School had a student body of only seventy-eight. The Nimrod basketball team, however, which competes in the Porcupine Mountain Conference, can draw crowds of up to twelve hundred for home games. Only fourteen hundred people reside in Watersmeet, so that's amazing support. Throughout the 1980s and 1990s, *nimrod* was a popular insult, referring to someone as a boob or idiot. But in reality, Nimrod is actually a biblical figure from the book of Genesis who was a mighty hunter. After the success of the ESPN campaign, Watersmeet High School was flooded with calls from across the country seeking shirts and hats bearing the Nimrods' name and their logo of a bearded hunter wearing a coonskin cap.[5]

Spirits of St. Louis (1974–1976)

The Spirits of St. Louis were members of the American Basketball Association. They took their name from Charles Lindbergh's famous single-seat monoplane the *Spirit of St. Louis*. In 1927 Lindbergh, a US Air Mail pilot, flew the plane solo on a nonstop flight from New York to Paris. He was the first to make such a trip and was hailed as a national hero for succeeding. Back then, it took Lindbergh thirty-three hours and thirty minutes to fly the thirty-six-hundred-mile distance. The Concorde jet could make the same trip in approximately three hours and forty-five minutes. The actual *Spirit of St. Louis* is currently on display in the National Air and Space Museum in Washington, DC.

Fun Fact: Did you know that North Carolina and Ohio have battled for years over which state should claim the heroics of Orville and Wilbur Wright, who in 1903 successfully piloted the first heavier-than-air flying machine? The flight took place in Kitty Hawk, North Carolina, because of its secluded location and steady winds. But the Wright brothers were bicycle mechanics from Dayton, Ohio. Though North Carolina has no major sports team that bears a nickname recognizing the Wright brothers' achievements, Ohio's University of Dayton Flyers do just that.

The Ohio State University Buckeyes

Residents of Ohio are often called Buckeyes. The Ohio State Buckeyes proudly represent that state university in sporting competitions. What exactly is a buckeye? It's a tree native to Ohio that produces a dark, shiny nut that resembles the eye of a deer. Yes, the university named its swift athletes after a rooted tree. That's because the tree is a particularly gritty one, growing in harsh places where others cannot. It's hard to destroy and adapts to difficult physical circumstances.[6] Hence, the people of Ohio view themselves to be as tough as that tree.

Dotting the i: Most football players on the Ohio State Buckeyes fantasize about scoring a game-winning touchdown. Members of their marching band have an equivalent dream. They dream of one day dotting the *i* when the band spells out *Ohio* in script on the field at halftime. It is all done with great precession and to overwhelming applause from the crowd. The honor is usually reserved for a senior sousaphone player.

CHALLENGE #13: CROSSING THE ATLANTIC—LINDBERGH VS. THE CONCORDE

How can we compute average miles per hour? Well, if a car made a 180-mile trip in three hours flat (and hopefully without one!), we would need to do some division to find the answer. We would divide the number of miles by time. Here, 180 miles divided by 3 hours equals 60 miles per hour. Now, Charles Lindbergh traveled 3,600 miles in 33.5 hours. How fast did he go? To get the answer, divide 3,600 by 33.5. (You may need a calculator.) Also, the Concorde jet traveled that same 3,600 miles in just 3.75 hours. How fast did the Concorde go? (You set up the formula for that one.) Finally, how much faster in miles per hour is the Concorde compared to the *Spirit of St. Louis*? (Use simple subtraction.)

TEXAS PRIDE

Dallas Cowboys (1960–present)

The NFL's Dallas Cowboys are named after the symbol of western freedom and independence—the working cowboy. Yes, a cowboy rides a horse, but his main job is herding and tending to cows, or cattle, on ranches. From 1866 to 1895, cowboys on horseback moved large herds over long distances to market on cattle drives. These Texas cattle drives usually headed to railway stations in Kansas, from which cattle could be shipped to stockyards in Chicago. Correspondingly, the University of Texas Longhorns are named after the famed Texas breed of cattle. Possessing lanky bodies and legs built for speed, the aggressive longhorns were able to survive treacherous cattle drives through blizzards, droughts, and dust storms.[7] Interestingly, the Dallas Cowboys were almost named the Steers by the team's original general manager, Tex Schramm.

Alternative Team Names: The Boys or America's Team (because of the Cowboys' extreme popularity outside of Texas); the University of Texas Longhorns are also referred to as the Horns.

© iStock/CCinspiration

Other Teams Named Cowboys: Oklahoma State University, McNeese State University (LA), New Mexico Highlands University, and the University of Wyoming, which has a silhouette of a cowboy riding a bucking bronco as its logo.

San Antonio Spurs (1973–present)

Upon the heels of their riding boots, cowboys often wore pointed metal spurs. These were designed to help riders move a horse forward or laterally. But spurs didn't get their start in the Old West. In fact, spurs can be traced all the way back to horsemen Celts in the fifth century BCE. More than one thousand years later, during medieval times, knights on horseback were said to have "earned their spurs" through victories in battle.[8] The NBA's San Antonio Spurs owe their sharp nickname to this enduring piece of riding equipment.

The Spurs began in the ABA, the league that introduced the three-point line and multicolored basketballs. They were originally named the Dallas Chaparrals. *Chaparral* is a Spanish word for a community of evergreen shrubs, bushes, and grasses. How did the original team owners choose that name? Through a complete lack of inspiration. It seems they had met at the Sheraton Dallas Hotel to, among other things, brainstorm a nickname for the fledgling franchise. After several hours, when nothing struck them, the owners decided to use the name of the conference room in which they were meeting—the Chaparral Room.[9]

Texas Rangers (1971–present)

MLB's Texas Rangers pay tribute to the oldest law enforcement agency in the United States. The Rangers policed Texas from 1830 to 1935, safeguarding the western frontiers from roving bandits, including gunfighter John Wesley Hardin and the infamous criminal duo Bonnie and Clyde. Perhaps the most recognizable Texas Ranger is the fictitious John Reid who, after donning his black mask, became better known as the Lone Ranger. He was accompanied by his faithful Native companion, Tonto, and his trusty steed Silver.

One Swift Kick: Martial arts icon Chuck Norris played the lead character Sergeant Cordell Walker in the television series *Walker, Texas Ranger*, which aired from 1993 to 2001. The six-time karate champion, beneath the brim of a wide cowboy hat, brought the bad guys to justice, usually after a spectacular fight scene.

Another Team Named Rangers: Hockey's New York Rangers, whose first logo pictured a blue horse carrying aloft a cowboy who waved a hockey stick.

Houston Colt .45s (1962-1964)/Houston Astros (1965-present)

The weapon made famous by the gun-toting Texas Rangers was the Colt .45 revolver, developed by Samuel Colt (1814-1862). Its power and accuracy gained it the reputation as "The Gun That Won the West." The Houston Colt .45s played baseball for three seasons before they were renamed the Houston Astros. During the 1960s, America was in a space race to become the first nation to land an astronaut on the moon. The Astros were named in recognition of NASA, which is based in Houston. Adding to their futuristic image, the Astros were the first franchise to play baseball indoors, as the Houston Astrodome became the forerunner of today's modern domed stadiums.

Alternative Team Name: Stros

Easy Move: Texas is referred to as the Lone Star State because of the one large star on the Texas state flag. It's the reason the Dallas Cowboys have a single star on the side of their football helmets. In 1993 hockey's Minnesota North Stars relocated to Dallas. In leaving Minnesota, which is called the North Star State, for Texas, the franchise simply dropped the word *North* from their nickname—hence, the now aptly renamed Dallas Stars.

CHALLENGE #14: CONTEXT CLUES

When you're not sure of the meaning of a particular word, you can often look at the surrounding words for help. This is called using context clues. Together, let's look at some vocabulary that appears in this chapter.

- *Treacherous:* We're told that longhorn cattle "were able to survive treacherous cattle drives through blizzards, droughts, and dust storms." Let's look at the context clues in that sentence—survive, blizzards, droughts, dust storms. Now you decide: Does treacherous mean safe or dangerous?
- *Infamous:* We're told that Bonnie and Clyde were an "infamous criminal duo." Let's look for the main context clue—criminal. Of course, there are some other clues scattered throughout the paragraph, such as bandits and gunfighter. Now you decide: Does infamous mean being well known for positive reasons or well known for negative reasons?

- *Enduring:* Okay, now you're on your own to find the context clues for spurs being an "enduring piece of riding equipment." Go back and look carefully for the clues throughout the paragraph. Does enduring mean modern and newly invented or having been around for a long period of time?

THE POLITICS OF SPORTS

Washington Nationals (2005–present)

Considering that Washington, DC, is the nation's capital, MLB's Washington Nationals are aptly named. That is, of course, when they get their own name correctly spelled. In 2009 the franchise sent two players onto the diamond in jerseys that were missing the letter "O." Instead of playing for the Nationals that night, the pair were members of the *Natinals*. It's usually baseball players who make errors on the field, but in this instance, it was the company that provided the uniforms. You think it's possible the pair of missing *O*s fell off in the wash-ington?

The Baltimore Orioles play baseball just outside of the Washington, DC, area. They are also known as the O's, short for Orioles. *Sensing an alphabetical pattern here?* The oriole is the official state bird of Maryland.

Alternative Team Name: The Nationals are also called the Nats.

Opening Day: Many US presidents have thrown out the ceremonial first pitch to begin the baseball season. But two presidents in particular have gotten even closer to the game. Ronald Reagan, the fortieth president, was once a sports announcer. He called Chicago Cubs games on radio. That was done from De Moines, Iowa—Reagan wasn't even present at the ballpark in Chicago. Instead, he was given the basic information via newswire and invented his own colorful play-by-play to accompany it. FYI: George W. Bush, the forty-third president, was actually a co-owner of the Texas Rangers baseball franchise.

President Gerald Ford, the thirty-eighth president, snapped the football at center while playing for the Michigan Wolverines from 1932 to 1934. Ford was voted his team's MVP in his final collegiate season. Also, the forty-fifth president, Donald J. Trump, owned a pro football team called the New Jersey Generals, which competed in the United States Football League.

Washington Capitals (1974–present)

The NHL's Washington Capitals are quite direct in their name. Prior to Washington, DC, becoming the nation's capital in 1800, several other cities served in that capacity. The list includes: Philadelphia (PA), New York City (NY), Annapolis (MD), Baltimore (MD), Trenton (NJ), and Princeton (NJ).

It's important to note the difference in spelling between *capital* and *capitol*, which is a building or group of buildings in which the government does its business. The United States Congress meets in the Capitol Building in Washington, DC, often called Capitol Hill.

Alternative Team Name: Caps

Washington Senators (1901–1960) and Ottawa Senators (1992–present)

MLB's former Washington Senators played in DC for six decades. The franchise drew its nickname from the Senate, which, along with the House of Representatives, makes up Congress, which assembles on Capitol Hill. There are a total of one hundred US senators—two elected from each state. A senator's term of office lasts six years. Among US senators who later became president are John F. Kennedy from Massachusetts and Barack Obama from Illinois.

In Canada, the government does business on Parliament Hill, located in Ottawa, Ontario. Canadian senators are not elected; instead, they are appointed by Canada's prime minister, and they can serve until the age of seventy-five. Since the city of Ottawa is the seat of its country's government, its NHL team is ideally named the Ottawa Senators.

Alternative Team Name: Both teams are also referred to as the Sens.
Other Teams Named Senators: Davis & Elkins College (WV). The Washington Senators (1921–1941) of pro football also went by the nicknames Pros and Presidents. The Tokyo Senators (1936–1939) of Japanese baseball folded at the start of World War II.

Army Black Knights, Navy Midshipmen, and Air Force Falcons

The fighting spirit is an essential part of the sports teams of the US service academies. The United States Military Academy at West Point—located in Orange County, New York, beside the Hudson River—is simply known in

© iStock/mitchellpictures

athletic circles as Army. The Army Black Knights received their nickname from their black uniforms.[10] The team has an intense football rivalry with the United States Naval Academy, located in Annapolis, Maryland. Navy's athletic teams have no official name, but they are widely recognized as the Navy Midshipmen. A *midshipman* is an officer or cadet of the junior-most rank. Not surprisingly, Navy's rallying cry is, "Beat Army!" The Army-Navy football game has been played annually since 1930. The United States Air Force Academy is in Colorado Springs, Colorado. The Air Force Falcons owe their nickname to the swift-winged birds of prey who kill with their sharp beaks instead of their talons and are native to the state.

Dictators and Baseball: Yes, they've played baseball in China for a long time—that is, whenever they're allowed. The Shanghai Baseball Club came into existence sometime prior to 1863. However, Mao Zedong (1893–1776), former chairman of the Communist Party, actually banned baseball in China because of its association with the West and freedom. The ban took effect in 1966 and lasted ten years, until Mao's death.[11]

In 1959 Fidel Castro (1926–2016) ditched his army fatigues and donned a baseball uniform to play an exhibition game for a team of revolutionaries nicknamed *Los Barbudos* (the Bearded Ones). Castro seized military and political power on the island nation of Cuba that same year, holding it for nearly six decades, until his death.

MARINE SCIENCES
AND METEOROLOGY

DEEP BLUE SEA

The state of Florida has a vast amount of coastline. That's because Florida is a peninsula—a piece of land that is bordered by water on three sides, but is connected to the mainland on the fourth. Florida has the Gulf of Mexico to its west, the Atlantic Ocean to its east, and the Straits of Florida to its south. In 1513 the ship of Spanish explorer Juan Ponce de Leon landed there, and he gave it the name *La Florida* (translated as "the flowery").[1] With all of that water dominating the scene, it's not surprising that several of the state's sports franchises are nicknamed after marine life.

Miami Dolphins (1966–present)

© NFL.com

The NFL's Miami Dolphins received their nickname through a fan contest. In 1972 the Dolphins recorded the NFL's only fully undefeated season, winning all fourteen regular-season games, two playoff games, and Super Bowl VII. Naturally, one of the team colors is aqua (water) blue. Though Dolphins live in the ocean, they aren't fish. They're actually mammals who give birth to live young and breathe oxygen. Their name comes from the Greek word *delphis*, which means "womb."[2] Dolphins are highly intelligent and social, living in groupings (often around one dozen) called *pods*. They communicate through high-pitched whistles that can be unique to the individual dolphin.

Alternative Team Names: Fins and Fish
Other Teams Named Dolphins: Jacksonville University (FL), California State University Channel Islands, College of Mount Saint Vincent (NY), and Sagrado Corazon University (Puerto Rico)

Miami Marlins (1993–present)

Florida is known for its incredible deep-sea fishing. One of its most sought-after conquests is the Atlantic blue marlin, which can weigh in at approximately eighteen hundred pounds and swim at speeds of 50 MPH. The marlin is easily recognized by its spearlike snout or bill and its long, rigid dorsal fin.[3] The fish is famous for the fierce fight it puts up once hooked. That fighting spirit inspired one of the state's baseball teams to call itself the Marlins.

In literature, Nobel Prize–winning author Ernest Hemingway penned a novel, *The Old Man and The Sea* (1952), in which a marlin is an essential character. In the book, an old Cuban fisherman named Santiago hooks a marlin full of fight, highlighting the intense struggle between man and nature.

Alternative Team Name: Fish
Another Team Named Marlins: Virginia Wesleyan University

Daytona Tortugas (2015–present)

The Daytona Tortugas, a Florida-based minor-league baseball team, figuratively speaking, only plays at home, never on the road. How so? In Spanish, *tortuga* means turtle or tortoise. So they always carry their *home* of a shell on their backs. Consider this: tortoises are turtles, but turtles aren't always tortoises. That's because turtles are shelled reptiles, while tortoises are land, or terrestrial, turtles that can't swim. Still, tortoises can hold their breath for a long time. Another fun fact: a grouping of tortoises is called a *creep*.[4]

Tampa Bay Devil Rays (1998–2007)/Tampa Bay Rays (2008–present)

The dictionary tells us that a team can be *bedeviled* (mercilessly tormented or plagued). But can a team be *un-deviled*? The Tampa Bay Devil Rays believed so. The team was originally named for an ocean fish called a *manta ray*. The manta ray is recognized for its wide body (as large as twenty-three feet wide), long spiked tails, and horn-shaped fins that gave it a devilish appearance. However, after a decade of futility on the baseball diamond, the franchise decided to change its fortunes by dropping the word *Devil* from its name. The Tampa Bay Rays are now named for the city's superb weather, as in bright rays of sunshine. Did changing the name affect their karma? In their first season as the Rays, the team made it all the way to the World Series, but lost. So you decide.

THE PACIFIC NORTHWEST

Seattle Mariners (1977-present)

The West Coast port city of Seattle, Washington, is built upon an isthmus—a narrow piece of land that connects two larger areas of land across an expanse of water. Seattle sits between Puget Sound and Lake Washington. Naturally, shipping and fishing are among the city's main sources of economic activity. It also serves as a gateway from the United States to the continent of Asia, which lies directly across the Pacific Ocean.[5] Seattle's Major League Baseball team is nicknamed the Mariners. A mariner is a person who directs or assists in the navigation of a ship. It is another name for a sailor. The city's previous MLB franchise was the short-lived Seattle Pilots, who played for only one season in 1969. Though most people think of a pilot as someone who flies an aircraft, it also refers to someone at the controls of a boat or ship.

A former member of the Seattle Pilots, pitcher Jim Bouton, wrote a tell-all book called *Ball Four* (1970), in which he detailed the private behind-the-scenes life of baseball players. As a result, many players of the era became angry with Bouton for breaking the code of not discussing the private lives of teammates.

Seattle Seahawks (1976-present)

In keeping with the ocean theme, Seattle's NFL franchise is nicknamed the Seahawks. A sea hawk is an osprey—a bird of prey that exclusively eats fish. Therefore, sea hawks—which can also be referred to as fish eagles, river hawks, or fish hawks—reside near bodies of water where fish are plentiful. This bird is

© iStock/Denja1

actually a species of raptor with sharp talons (feet/claws) that enable it to firmly grasp and fly away with its catch.[6] You can go online to watch the majestic sea hawk or osprey fish a body of water.

Prior to Super Bowl XLVIII in 2013, the Washington State Senate, for a short time, renamed Mount Rainier—the tallest mountain in the state and an active volcano—Mount Seahawk. It must have inspired confidence in the team, because the Seahawks crushed the Denver Broncos, 43–8, to earn their first championship.

Alternative Team Names: Hawks, Blue Wave, and Legion of Boom (for their hard-hitting secondary on defense)

Seattle Sounders (1994–present), Seattle Storm (2000–present), and Seattle Reign (2012–present)

Seattle boasts a trio of other water-inspired nicknames. The city sits on the Puget Sound, which extends approximately one hundred miles and is home to incredible marine life such as harbor seals, orca, salmon, and trout. The sound is such a vital part of the surroundings that the Seattle Sounders are the city's representative in Major League Soccer. Seattle is also known for staggering amounts of rainfall, or precipitation, during its cool, wet winters. It is routinely among the five rainiest US cities, and also ranks high among US cities with the lowest amount of annual sunshine. That type of climate inspired the WNBA's Seattle Storm. Not to be outdone, the city's entrant in the National Women's Soccer League sports a beautiful play on words: the Seattle Reign. Unlike *rain*, or precipitation, *reign* means the amount of time someone such as a king or queen holds royal office—or, figuratively, how long a sports team remains on top of the standings.

Community Colleges of Spokane Sasquatch

The system of community colleges in Spokane, Washington, has nicknamed its athletic teams the Sasquatch, after the mythical apelike creature that walks upright like a man. The towering creature has long been associated with the forests and wilderness of the Pacific Northwest. Many people have claimed to see a Sasquatch, pointing to huge footprints left behind as evidence. Because of these large prints, the Sasquatch is also called Big Foot. Do you believe this creature actually exists?

HOT STREAKS

Phoenix Suns (1968–present) and Phoenix Mercury (1997–present)

The city of Phoenix, Arizona, originally had a difficult time getting an NBA franchise due to its desert climate. The conventional thinking was that Phoenix, which is called the Valley of the Sun, was simply too hot to support a basketball team. Phoenix's daily high temperature over the summer months easily exceeds 100 degrees Fahrenheit. In fact, the city's record-high temperature was recorded at 122 degrees. Phoenix receives little rainfall and averages more than 330 days of sunshine annually. (That's 90 percent of the year.)[7] But don't believe the area is all cacti and desert sands. Phoenix is situated between the Salt River and the Gila River, and the ground is fertile enough to make the farming of citrus and cotton a major part of its economy. When it came time to choose a nickname for its hoops team, the city's climate was totally embraced, giving birth to the Phoenix Suns.

Similarly, the city's WNBA franchise is named the Phoenix Mercury. Mercury is a chemical element designated by the symbol Hg on the Periodic Table of Elements. It is also known as *quicksilver* because of the speed at which it moves, being the only metallic element that is a liquid. Perhaps its most common use is as a measuring element inside of a glass thermometer.

Miami Heat (1988–present) and Miami Sol (2000–2002)

© NBA.com

Rivaling Phoenix for the highest daily temperature for a US city is Miami, Florida. Miami is located along the Atlantic shore and has extremely hot and humid summers. The tropical climate causes plenty of afternoon thunderstorms helping to cool things down, although the city of Miami has never officially recorded any snowfall. Miami's NBA team is smartly called the Heat. Its counterpart in the WNBA was nicknamed the Miami Sol. In Spanish, *sol* means "sun." The name also reflected Miami's large Latino population.

Olmecas de Tabasco (1975–present)

Olmecas de Tabasco is a minor-league baseball team based in the Mexican state of Tabasco. The Olmecas are the earliest known civilization in Mexico, from about 1500 to 400 BCE—notice the years are getting smaller, not larger—and are famous for their artwork of colossal stone heads.[8] You're correct: the Mexican state of Tabasco is the namesake of tabasco sauce, because the tabasco pepper grows there. The sauce itself, though, is not made in Mexico. Rather, it is a product originally bottled in Avery Island, Louisiana.

STORM WARNINGS

Carolina Hurricanes (1997–present)

A hurricane is a tropical cyclone—a rapidly rotating storm system with a low-pressure center (the eye), strong winds, and thunderstorms. Hurricanes receive their energy through the evaporation of water from the ocean surface, which ultimately re-forms into clouds and rain as the moist air rises. That's why hurricanes typically weaken over land, where they are cut off from their energy source.[9] Hurricanes occur in the North Atlantic and the Northeast Pacific. In the Northwest Pacific, these same storms are called *typhoons*.

Hurricanes in the United States typically strike the East Coast from the Carolinas to Florida during hurricane season, which runs from June 1 through November 30. The NHL's Carolina Hurricanes call the city of Raleigh, North Carolina, home. Over the years, more than four hundred hurricanes have wreaked havoc in the state, causing serious damage and even loss of life. The fierce storms are given names—alphabetically—in alternating male/female order.

Here are the names given to Hurricanes in 2019: Andrea, Barry, Chantal, Dorian, Erin, Fernand, Gabrielle . . . You can go online to research the rest and find out if your name is on this or future lists.

Other teams with stormy nicknames include the Iowa State Cyclones and the University of New England Nor'easters. Of course, lopsided wins or losses by wind-inspired nicknames can be described as blowouts.

Alternative Team Name: Canes
Other Teams Named Hurricanes: University of Miami (FL) and Georgia Southwestern State University

Oklahoma City Thunder (2008–present)

The NBA's Thunder has an ideal nickname for their place of residence. The name was chosen because the state of Oklahoma is the frequent site of powerful thunderstorms in a stretch of the central United States where many tornadoes hit. A tornado is a violently rotating column of funnel-like air, with the narrow end touching the earth. It evolved from the Spanish word *tronada*, meaning "thunderstorm." Oklahoma City is also home to the 45th Infantry Division of the US Army, which is called the Thunderbirds.

Other Teams Named Thunder: Lake Erie College (OH), Trine University (IN), and Wheaton College (IL)

CHALLENGE #15: TEAM NAMES THAT DON'T END IN *S*

Most team nicknames end with the letter *s*. In this chapter, however, four of the teams we discussed do not. They are the Miami Heat, Miami Sol, Phoenix Mercury, and Oklahoma City Thunder. Now, go back through the preceding chapters of this text and see how many other teams you can find without an *s* at the end of their names. What letters do they most commonly end in? Are they vowels or consonants?

12

ELECTIVES AND INDEPENDENT STUDIES

A PALETTE OF COMPETING COLORS

Cincinnati Reds (1881–present)

© MLB.com

B aseball as we know it today was formulated through a set of rules published in 1845 by an amateur club called the New York Knickerbockers. Those rules included: nine players on a team, nine-inning games, and bases ninety feet apart (the same as modern-day baseball). The new rules also eliminated plugging—the act of achieving an out by hitting the runner with the ball.[1] The first professional team was the Cincinnati Red Stockings, who played from 1869 to 1875. Major League Baseball's Cincinnati Reds can trace their heritage all the way back to that initial pro squad. The team received its name because the players wore red baseball stockings. The team's moniker has undergone slight changes over the years. The Red Stockings became the Redlegs and then finally the Reds. But for a brief time during the 1950s, when communism was seen as a threat to the American way of life (communists were called Reds because of the Soviet Union's red flag), the franchise actually removed the word *Reds* from the uniform.[2]

Alternative Team Name: Big Red Machine (inspired by the championship Reds teams of the mid-1970s)

Boston Red Sox and Chicago White Sox (both 1901–present)

A baseball team began in Boston in 1901 without an official nickname. That team wore dark blue socks. But in 1907, after the league switched to white uniforms for all teams, the franchise decided that red would stand out quite nicely against it. Hence, the Boston Red Sox were born a season later.[3] And *Sox* fit more neatly than *Stockings* into a newspaper headline.

The Chicago White Sox were also named for the color of their hosiery. The 1919 version of the team, however, was infamously dubbed the Black Sox because eight of their members were accused of purposely losing the World Series that year to the Cincinnati Reds. Although they were acquitted (found innocent in a court of law) of those charges, all eight players were banned from baseball for life by the commissioner. The plots of a pair of Hollywood films—*Eight Men Out* (1988) and *Field of Dreams* (1989)—dramatically explore the Black Sox scandal.

The Red Sox play their home games at Fenway Park. The stadium's distinguishing mark, however, isn't red. Rather, it's green. The left field wall, which stands 37.2 feet in height, is referred to as the Green Monster.

Comiskey Park was the home of the White Sox from 1910 until 1990. That's where owner Bill Veeck decided to stage Disco Demolition Night on July 12, 1979. The promotion featured blowing up a crate of disco records between games of a doubleheader. But the resulting explosion and the rowdy fans, who rushed onto the field afterward, caused such damage to the field that the White Sox were forced to forfeit the second game.

Alternative Team Names: The Red Sox are also called the Sox and BoSox. The White Sox are also called ChiSox, Southsiders (because they play on the South Side of Chicago), and Pale Hose.

Cleveland Browns (1946–1995) (1999–present)

The Cleveland Browns football franchise was named after their first head coach, Paul Brown, making the team another sports eponym. Coincidentally, perhaps the greatest football player to ever set foot on a field was also named Brown. That would be Hall of Fame running back Jim Brown. And as fate would have it, Jim Brown was drafted by the Cleveland Browns in 1957. Brown played his entire nine-year career with the Browns, leading them to the NFL championship in 1964.

University of Alabama Crimson Tide, Stanford University Cardinal, and St. Louis Cardinals (1900–present)

The University of Alabama Crimson Tide, the Stanford University Cardinal, and even baseball's St. Louis Cardinals are all named for their team's colors. Alabama used to be called the Thin Red Line until they played an inspiring football game one day in a sea of red mud and a sportswriter renamed them the Crimson Tide.[4] Stanford University used to be called the Indians until protests at the school led to a name change. They ultimately adopted Cardinal (a shade of red). And despite having their modern jerseys adorned with songbirds, the St. Louis Cardinals originally received their nickname for the vivid red color of their uniforms.

Alternate Team Names: The St. Louis Cardinals are often referred to as the Cards, Redbirds, and Birds.

Other Teams Named Cardinals: The NFL's Arizona Cardinals, who were previously the Chicago Cardinals (1920–1956) and St. Louis Cardinals (1960–1987); also, Ball State University (IN), University of Louisville (KY), Lamar University (TX), and Wesleyan (CT)

Off-Key Victory: The Stanford Cardinal football team will forever be remembered for its 1982 marching band. That's because during a last-second kickoff against their rivals the California Golden Bears, the Stanford band came onto the field, believing the game clock had expired. It hadn't. The band got in the way of their own defenders trying to tackle the kick returner (after several laterals between Golden Bears). The final Cal ballcarrier, zig-zagging through band members, found his way into the end zone, knocking a trombone player flat for good measure. "The Play," as it has since been dubbed, provided Cal a heart-stopping 25–20 triumph.

Run, Forrest, Run: In the 1994 film *Forrest Gump*, actor Tom Hanks, who plays Forrest, runs a kickoff back for a touchdown as a member of the Alabama Crimson Tide football team. As their legions of fans would say, "Roll Tide!"

TENNIS ANYONE?

Chicago Aces (1974), Boston Lobsters (1975–1978), Detroit/Indiana Loves (1974–1978), and Hawaii Leis (1974–1976)

The modern game of tennis originated in Birmingham, England, in the nineteenth century. It was known as *lawn tennis* and was played on grass. Nowadays, people mostly think of tennis as an individual sport, unless you play doubles competition. But from 1974 to 1978, many of the world's greatest tennis players, such as Billie Jean King, Chris Evert, Bjorn Borg, and Jimmy Connors, competed on teams in a league called World Team Tennis (WTT). Naturally, each team had a home city and a nickname. The Chicago Aces were named for the tennis term *ace*, hitting a serve that can't be returned by an opponent. The Boston Lobsters sported a nickname with a dual meaning: Lobsters from the sea are a tasty catch in the New England area, but a *lobster* is also a piece of tennis equipment that automatically fires balls over the net so you can practice alone. The Detroit/Indiana Loves were named for the tennis term *love*, which represents a zero when keeping score: for example, I'm losing this set, five games to love (zero). The Hawaii Leis were inspired by the necklace of flowers given to visitors as a symbol of affection in the Hawaiian culture.

© WTT.com

Philadelphia Freedoms (1974–1975)

Perhaps the most memorable team in WTT turned out to be the Philadelphia Freedoms. Yes, the Freedoms get their name from the American Revolution of 1776 and the city's important role in that event. But musician Elton John was a close friend of Freedoms star Billie Jean King, who had fought tenaciously to get women on the pro tennis circuit the same prize money as men. So John, along with his musical collaborator, Bernie Taupin, penned a hit song entitled "Philadelphia Freedom" (1975), boosting the team's exposure and cool factor.

Go online to hear Elton John perform "Philadelphia Freedom."

Idaho Sneakers (1994)

You'd think there would be at least several teams in various sports named after types of athletic shoes. But there aren't. Instead, we only have one representative—the very simple and straightforward Idaho Sneakers of WTT. If this franchise were still around today, would major shoe companies like Nike, Adidas, and Fila be fighting to have the Sneakers wear their product?

JUST FOR FUN

Scottsdale Community College
Fighting Artichokes

In the early 1970s, the administration at Scottsdale Community College in Arizona asked its students to vote on a new name for its football team. Many of the students believed the school was putting too much money into athletics and not enough into education. So in protest, they responded by picking the name Fighting Artichokes. The administration tried to ignore their choice, but the students wouldn't relent. A second election was held and the Fighting Artichokes was the overwhelming winner.[5] Today the name, along with the school's mascot, Artie the Artichoke—originally intended to shame the administration—is now a source of local pride. The artichoke is a species of thistle cultivated for food. The country of Italy is the largest producer of the artichokes, growing more than five hundred tons each year.

Of course, other schools have followed suit in choosing fun, food-inspired nicknames. This includes the Fighting Pickle of the University of North Carolina School of the Arts. That's *Pickle*, singular. There's also the Fighting Okra of Delta State University in Cleveland, Mississippi. The school's real name is the Statesmen, but the student body believed that no opponent would find that intimidating, so they adopted the image of a pugilistic green flowering plant instead. Go figure. And don't forget the Tokyo University of Agriculture Fighting Radish in Japan.

Contradiction in Terms: Minor-league baseball's Jacksonville Jumbo Shrimp is a prime example of an oxymoron. *What did you call me?* It's not an insult; it's a device that reveals a contradiction in terms or a paradox—in this case, because shrimp are supposed to be small. On the flip side, there's the Little Giants of Wabash College in Indiana.

Akron Rubber Ducks (2014–present)

The iconic yellow rubber duck first appeared in the 1940s. Since then, more than 50 million have been sold.[6] Rubber duck races to raise funds for charities are now staged worldwide. One of the biggest is the Rubber Duck Regatta held annually in Cincinnati, Ohio. Another city in Ohio—Akron—has gone one step further in showing its appreciation by hosting a minor-league baseball team nicknamed the Rubber Ducks. Why the connection to the state of Ohio? Well, Akron is the birthplace of tire and rubber companies such as Firestone, Goodrich, and Goodyear.

You can go online to see rubber duck races or to hear *Sesame Street*'s Ernie sing his classic song, "Rubber Duckie."

Saint Louis University Billikens

Early in the twentieth century, Billiken dolls were all the rage. In fact, they were a fad (a short-lived craze). Lots of people decided they desperately needed to have one. The dolls supposedly brought good luck. They were good luck to buy, and even better luck to receive as a gift. Now that's a marketing strategy! Thus, the University of St. Louis adopted Billikens as the nickname for its athletic teams. So you can refer to them as the luckiest teams in collegiate sports.

Here are examples of other twentieth-century fads: Pet Rocks, Mood Rings, Cabbage Patch Dolls, and Fidget Spinners. How many do you remember? What's the difference between a fad and a trend? Trends usually have much longer life spans.

Molecules, Molecules: The St. Louis College of Pharmacy Eutectics sport athletic teams with plenty of chemistry. How so? And what is a eutectic? Well, it's the scientific process of a pair of solids combining to form a liquid. *Rah! Rah! Science!*

COLLEGE QUESTION MARKS

Here are some fun questions to consider in the scheduling of intercollegiate matchups:

- Shouldn't the Mules (Central Missouri State) post a stubborn victory over the Mule Riders (Southern Arkansas University)?
- In a matchup between the Lumberjacks (Northern Arizona University) and the Sycamores (Indiana State University), would the Lumberjacks have the edge?

- Can you imagine a basketball game between the Frogs (Hampshire College) and Kangaroos (Austin College)? Think about the jump ball!
- Shouldn't the Owls (Temple University) only schedule night games?
- Why did the tournament between the Bonnies (St. Bonaventure), Jimmies (St. James College), Johnnies (St. John's), and Tommies (University of St. Thomas) have to be cancelled? Answer: Their mothers wouldn't let them out to play.
- Shouldn't the Pilgrims (New England College) and the Gobblers (Virginia Tech's former mascot) play each other every Thanksgiving Day?
- Why is it that the Zips (University of Akron) are constantly getting shut out?
- Aren't the Matadors (California State University, Northridge) and Toros (California State University, Dominguez Hills) natural rivals?

THIRD AND FINAL OFFICIAL TIMEOUT: BUILDING YOUR OWN SPORTS FRANCHISE IN HARTFORD, CONNECTICUT

Okay, here's our third and final official timeout!

During our second timeout, you were given a chance to name a brand-new sports team for the city of Wichita, Kansas. For this assignment we're headed east, to the state of Connecticut and its capital city of Hartford. You can choose either the state or the city to begin your team's name. Feel free to select the sport for your team. Or create multiple teams and their nicknames to play in this region.

This time around, consider creating your own team mascot and a team logo. Maybe you're good at drawing or can create images on a computer. Maybe you have a talented friend or sibling with whom you could partner, allowing them to become co-owner of this team with you.

Here's the background you'll need on the region to begin:

The capital city of Hartford is among the largest in the state of Connecticut. Hartford is often referred to as the Insurance Capital of the World because of the many insurance companies whose main offices are located there. It is also home to the Mark Twain House, where the famous writer Samuel Langhorne Clemens (aka Mark Twain) lived and penned some of his classic works, including *The Adventures of Tom Sawyer*, *Adventures of Huckleberry Finn*, and *A Connecticut Yankee in King Arthur's Court*.

In the mid-nineteenth century, inventor Samuel Colt started a company in Hartford to build his continuous-firing .45 Colt revolver, often called "The Gun That Won the West." Prior to the American Civil War, Hartford was also

© iStock/Ultima_Gaina

a center for abolitionists—people involved in the movement to end slavery in the United States. Hartford was once home to an NHL hockey franchise, the Hartford Whalers, who played there from 1979 to 1997. The team was named to honor the tradition of whaling ships that left from the port cities of New England to hunt whales.

Connecticut is known as the Nutmeg State. Nutmeg is a spice created from several species of trees. However, those trees are not native to the state. During the eighteenth and nineteenth centuries, sailors brought the valuable spice back from their foreign voyages. Those sailors were often accused of selling fake nutmeg seeds made out of wood to scam a hefty profit.[7] The name Connecticut is derived from a Native American word meaning a "long tidal river."[8] The state actually received its name from the Connecticut River, the longest in the New England region. Connecticut is also part of the Tri-State Area, along with New York and New Jersey. The state is also known for its bountiful harvest of oysters, in which beautiful and valuable pearls can sometimes be found. Currently, the WNBA's Connecticut Sun is the state's only pro sports team. Their nickname comes from an affiliation with the Mohegan Sun Casino, operated by a Native American tribe. Among the famous people born in the state are patriot Nathan Hale, who said, "I only regret that I have but one life to lose for my country"; and Noah Webster, who helped create the modern dictionary, *An American Dictionary of the English Language*, published in 1828.

I hope that's enough information on the state of Connecticut and its capital city of Hartford to get your brain thinking and creative juices flowing! Don't forget to create yourself a deed for your new team—an important piece of paper that shows:

1. Ownership
2. Team nickname
3. Type of sport
4. Stadium or arena name
5. Name and description of mascot
6. Description and drawing of your team's logo

Congratulations on becoming a franchise owner! You've earned it through the fun and learning you experienced in these many chapters. I hope your team takes root in the heart of the city and state in which it plays. And I hope your team's nickname becomes as much a part of its fans' lives as the teams we learned about in the pages of this book.

CHALLENGE ANSWERS

CHALLENGE #1: LESS VIOLENT LANGUAGE

In removing violent imagery from the game recap, here are the words you should have focused on eliminating: *slaughter* (from the headline), *battered, assaulted, attack, ripped, struck, walloping, killed, whipping, slapped,* and *beating*. That passage was fairly violent, wasn't it?

CHALLENGE #2: DATING THE CENTURY

The year 912 is the tenth century. 1389 is the fourteenth century. 1755 is the eighteenth century. 1965 is the twentieth century. And finally, 2014 is the twenty-first century.

CHALLENGE #3: ROMAN NUMERALS AND THE SUPER BOWL

Super Bowl XXIII is number 23. Super Bowl XXIV is number 24. And Super Bowl XXIX is number 29. Wow, those San Francisco 49ers have a lot of championship rings!

CHALLENGE #7: ALLITERATIVE NAMES

Some of the alliterated team names are: San Antonio Spurs, Seattle Supersonics, Edmonton Eskimos, Los Angeles Lakers, and Buffalo Bills. There are many others. Keep looking.

CHALLENGE #8: STATE CAPITALS NAMED FOR US PRESIDENTS

In addition to Nebraska—Lincoln—Abraham Lincoln,

Missouri—Jefferson City—Thomas Jefferson
Mississippi—Jackson—Andrew Jackson
Wisconsin—Madison—James Madison

CHALLENGE #9: CHANGING MILLIONS INTO BILLIONS

1.3 billion is numerically written as 1,300,000,000.

CHALLENGE #10: HOW MANY LAPS TO A MILE?

200 Laps.

CHALLENGE #12: PUNCTUATION AND MEANING

Careful, man-eating tiger
You will need to work twenty-four hour shifts. = 24 hours
You will need to work twenty four-hour shifts. = 80 hours

CHALLENGE # 13: CROSSING THE ATLANTIC—LINDBERGH VS. THE CONCORDE

Lindbergh traveled at an average speed of 107.46 miles per hour.
The Concorde traveled at an average speed of 960 miles per hour.
The Concorde is 852.54 miles per hour faster.

CHALLENGE #14: CONTEXT CLUES

Treacherous means dangerous.
Infamous means well-known for negative reasons.
Enduring means having been around for a long period of time.

CHALLENGE #15: TEAM NAMES THAT DON'T END IN *S*

Most teams with singular names end in consonants. Some examples are: Bison, Buzz, Cardinal, Crush, Jazz, Shrimp, Magic, and Mayhem.

Now, sometimes a *y* takes the place of the ending vowel. The Mutiny is a good example of this.

The silent *e* also gets us there with teams such as: Avalanche, Curve, Pickle, and Courage.

NOTES

CHAPTER 1: WORLD HISTORY

1. Roger Treat, *The Encyclopedia of Football* (New York: Barnes, 1974), 15–16.

2. Rutgers University Athletics, "The First Game: Nov. 6, 1869," https://scarlet knights.com/sports/2017/6/11/sports-m-footbl-archive-first-game-html.aspx (August 10, 2017).

3. The Way of the Pirates, "Viking Pirates," www.thewayofthepirates.com/types -of-pirates/viking-pirates (September 25, 2018).

4. Harry Atkins, "Ten Facts about Viking Longships" History Hit, May 11, 2018, www.historyhit.com/facts-about-viking-longships (August 15, 2018).

5. Football Babble, "NFL Fight Songs," www.footballbabble.com/football/nfl/ fight-songs (September 1, 2018).

6. Ben Goessling, "Prince Penned 'Purple and Gold' Fight Song for Vikings in 2010," ESPN.com, April 21, 2016, www.espn.com/blog/minnesota-vikings/post/_/ id/18649/prince-penned-purple-and-gold-fight-song-for-vikings-in-2010 (September 1, 2018).

7. Online Etymology Dictionary, "Buccaneer," www.etymonline.com/word/ buccaneer (August 5, 2018).

8. Tim Beattie, *British Privateering Voyages of the Early Eighteenth Century* (Woodbridge, Suffolk, UK: Boydell & Brewer, 2015), 54.

9. Joseph Alexander, *Edson's Raiders: The 1st Marine Raider Battalion in World War II Maryland* (Annapolis, MD: Naval Institute Press, 2000), 14–15.

10. Chris Potter, "Why Is Our Baseball Team Called the Pittsburgh Pirates? What Do Pirates Have to Do with Pittsburgh?" *Pittsburgh City Paper*, August 14, 2003, www .pghcitypaper.com/pittsburgh/why-is-our-baseball-team-called-the-pittsburgh-pirates -what-do-pirates-have-to-do-with-pittsburgh/Content?oid=1335541 (August 10, 2018).

11. Infoplease, "Honus Wagner," www.infoplease.com/encyclopedia/people/sports-and-games/sports-biographies/wagner-honus (July 16, 2017).

12. Melissa Rohlin, "Nuns Sell Baseball Card for $262,000," *Los Angeles Times*, November 5, 2010, http://latimesblogs.latimes.com/sports_blog/2010/11/nuns-sell -baseball-card-for-262000.html (September 30, 2018).

13. Karl Wuensch, "Blackbeard and Pee Dee," East Carolina University, http://core .ecu.edu/psyc/wuenschk/Blackbeard.htm (May 18, 2017).

14. Encyclopaedia Britannica, "Jean Lafitte: American Pirate," www.britannica .com/biography/Jean-Laffite (May 11, 2017).

15. The Way of the Pirates, "Famous Privateer: Jean Lafitte," www.thewayofthe pirates.com/famous-privateers/jean-laffite (April 10, 2017).

16. Dan Steinberg, "Why Abe Pollin Went from Bullets to Wizards," *Washing-ton Post*, February 2, 2010, http://voices.washingtonpost.com/dcsportsbog/2010/02/ why_abe_pollin_went_from_bulle.html (April 5, 2017).

17. Owen Jarus, "History of the Celts," Live Science, April 7, 2014, www.live science.com/44666-history-of-the-celts.html (January 14, 2017).

18. Brendan O'Shaughnessy, "What's in a Name? How Notre Dame became the Fighting Irish," University of Notre Dame, www.nd.edu/features/whats-in-a-name (May 15, 2017).

19. United States History, "Quakers," www.u-s-history.com/pages/h486.html (June 9, 2017).

20. Dennis Jarvis, "Aztec Sun Stone," Ancient History Encyclopedia, September 4, 2013, www.ancient.eu/image/1416/aztec-sun-stone (August 25, 2016).

21. University of Hawaii Athletics, "U of H Traditions," https://hawaiiathletics.com/ sports/2012/6/18/GEN_0618120234.aspx (August 22, 2017).

CHAPTER 2: AMERICAN HISTORY

1. The "Cowboys Finish off Redskins" headline is noted on the website American Indian Sports Team Mascots, https://aistm.org (January 15, 2017).

2. Earl Perkins, "The Chief Whose Time Has Passed," *Thursday Review*, July 10, 2014, www.thursdayreview.com/Noc-A-Homa.html (January 17, 2017).

3. "Indians History Overview," MLB.com, http://cleveland.indians.mlb.com/cle/ history/cle_history_overview.jsp (January 23, 2017).

4. "Chicago Blackhawks," Team Name Origin, http://teamnameorigin.com/nhl/ nickname/chicago-blackhawks (August 12, 2018).

5. James Lewis, "Black Hawk," *Encyclopedia Britannica*, last updated January 16, 2018, www.britannica.com/biography/Black-Hawk-Sauk-and-Fox-leader (August 29, 2018).

6. "Survival in the Swamp," Seminole Tribe of Florida, www.semtribe.com/STOF/ history/survival-in-the-swamp (August 15, 2017).

7. Roger Treat, *The Encyclopedia of Football* (New York, Barnes, 1974), 37.

8. "Declaration of Independence," History Channel, October 27, 2009, www .history.com/topics/american-revolution/declaration-of-independence (August 5, 2017).

9. "Sons and Daughters of Liberty," *American Revolution* (blog), February 4, 2011, http://theamrevolution.blogspot.com/2011/02/sons-and-daughters-of-liberty .html (July 31, 2017).

10. "Charlotte History 10 Things to Know," Levine Museum of the New South, 2018, http://web.archive.org/web/20180728170358/https://www.museumofthenew south.org/learn/history-resources/charlotte-history-10-things-to-know (August 5, 2018).

11. "California History: The Gold Rush," California State Library, http://library .ca.gov/california-history/gold-rush (May 15, 2017).

12. "Gold (AU)," Lenntech, www.lenntech.com/periodic/elements/au.htm (June 17, 2017).

13. "Chicago Fire of 1871," History Channel, March 4, 2010, www.history.com/ topics/19th-century/great-chicago-fire (August 14, 2018).

14. Stephen Robertson, "Basketball in 1920s Harlem," *Digital Harlem* (blog), June 3, 2011, https://digitalharlemblog.wordpress.com/2011/06/03/basketball-in-1920s -harlem (August 1, 2018).

15. Stan Hoig, "Land Run of 1889" *Encyclopedia of Oklahoma History and Culture*, www.okhistory.org/publications/enc/entry.php?entry=LA014 (June 19, 2018).

CHAPTER 3: LITERATURE, LANGUAGE, AND MYTHOLOGY

1. "Exploration to Statehood," Ohio History Central, http://ohiohistorycentral .org/w/Category:Exploration_To_Statehood?rec=2 (May 27, 2017).

2. "Boston Bruins: How Did They Get Their Name?" *Sports Then and Now* (blog), April 3, 2011, http://boston.sportsthenandnow.com/2011/04/03/boston-bruins-how -did-they-get-their-name (August 5, 2017).

3. "Bruin," Memidex, www.memidex.com/bruin (August 7, 2017).

4. "History of Brampton Lacrosse and the Minors," Brampton Minor Lacrosse As-sociation, www.bramptonlacrosse.ca/page/show/284644-history-of-brampton-lacrosse -and-the-minors (July 24, 2017).

5. "Whittier College History," Whittier College, www.whittier.edu/about/history (August 5, 2017).

6. "Franchise Timeline: Dodgers," MLB.com, http://losangeles.dodgers.mlb.com/ la/history/timeline.jsp (August 30, 2018).

7. "Georgetown Traditions: What's a Hoya?" HoyaSaxa.com, www.hoyasaxa.com/ sports/hoia.htm (May 12, 2107).

8. Jennie Cohen, "Super Bowl Owes Its Name to a Bouncy Ball," History Channel, February 3, 2012, www.history.com/news/super-bowl-owes-its-name-to-a-bouncy-ball (November 25, 2017).

9. Kenneth Ronkowitz, "Montreal Expos," *Why Name It That?* (blog), August 29, 2016, http://whynameitthat.blogspot.com/2016/08/montreal-expos.html (July 23, 2017).

10. "World Famous Horseshoe Curve," Railroaders Memorial Museum, www.railroadcity.com/visit/world-famous-horseshoe-curve (August 9, 2017).

11. "What Is a Boilermaker?" Purdue Sports, www.purduesports.com/trads/what-is-boilermaker.html (September 30, 2018).

12. "What's a Knickerbocker?" NBA.com, www.nba.com/knicks/history/what saknickerbocker.html (May 10, 2017).

13. "Yankee," Online Etymology Dictionary, www.etymonline.com/word/yankee (September 5, 2018).

14. "Mavericks," AlphaDictionary.com, www.alphadictionary.com/articles/eponyms/eponym_list_m.html (August 5, 2017).

15. "Why Is North Carolina Called the Tar Heel State?" *WiseGeek.com* 2017, www.wisegeek.com/why-is-north-carolina-called-the-tar-heel-state.htm#didyouknowout (September 5, 2018).

16. "Tar," MerriamWebster.com, www.merriam-webster.com/dictionary/tar (October 1, 2018).

17. "About Us: 1872–1879," Argonaut Rowing Club, https://web.archive.org/web/20130310122253/http://www.argonautrowingclub.com/Content/About%20Us/Club.asp (September 30, 2018).

18. Bob Henderson, "Athens of the South," Athens-South.com, https://athens-south.com/athens-of-the-south (September 26, 2017).

19. "The Origins of the Legendary Griffin," Ancient Origins, www.ancient-origins.net/myths-legends/ancient-origins-legendary-griffin-001693 (September 1, 2017).

20. "Birth of the Elon Phoenix," Elon Phoenix: The Official Site of Elon University Athletics, https://elonphoenix.com (September 30, 2018).

CHAPTER 4: MUSIC AND POP CULTURE

1. "James Naismith and the Invention of Basketball," Jr. NBA.com, https://jr.nba.com/james-naismith-invention-basketball (September 8, 2018).

2. "Allan Freed Biography," Rock & Roll Hall of Fame, www.rockhall.com/inductees/alan-freed (September 9, 2018).

3. "History of Jazz," Scholastic.com, http://teacher.scholastic.com/activities/bhistory/history_of_jazz.htm (September 8, 2018).

4. "W. C. Handy," Biography.com, www.biography.com/people/wc-handy-39700 (August 17, 2018).

5. "New Orleans Saints," Team Name Origin, http://teamnameorigin.com/nfl/nickname/new-orleans-saints (July 29, 2108).

6. Robert Silva, "The Nashville Sound Explained," ThoughtCo.com, March 29, 2017, www.thoughtco.com/the-nashville-sound-explained-931989 (September 17, 2018).

7. "How Many Lakes Does Minnesota Actually Have?" Reference.com, www .reference.com/geography/many-lakes-minnesota-actually-33b3246b3220ee57 (June 21, 2018).

8. "Origin of 'Minnesota,'" State Symbols USA, https://statesymbolsusa.org/ symbol-official-item/minnesota/state-name-origin/origin-minnesota (August 6, 2017).

9. "Behind the Name: Orlando Magic," NBA.com, www.nba.com/magic/news/ behindthename.html (September 1, 2017).

10. "Magic Kingdom Facts," Ron & Marie's Disney Trivia, www.disneytrivia.net/ park_pages/wdw_mk_facts.php (September 2, 2018).

11. "History of the Harlem Globetrotters," Timetoast, www.timetoast.com/timelines/ the-history-of-the-harlem-globetrotters (August 1, 2018).

12. Jay Smith, "The Harlem Globetrotters," *Chicago Stories*, WTTW, 2007, https:// interactive.wttw.com/a/chicago-stories-harlem-globetrotters (December 21, 2018).

13. Tim Povtak, "Dream Team Dazzles in Laugher," *Orlando Sentinel*, June 29, 1992, http://articles.orlandosentinel.com/1992-06-29/sports/9206290292_1_dream -team-cuba-clyde-drexler (September 10, 2018).

14. "Bulls History," MiLB.com, www.milb.com/content/page.jsp?sid=t234&ymd =20110803&content_id=22698520&vkey=team3 (September 1, 2018).

15. Chris Wright, "Hit Bull Win Steak," *Raleigh News & Observer*, August 16, 2015, www.newsobserver.com/sports/article31247435.html (August 29, 2018).

16. "Arkansas," National Park Service, www.nps.gov/state/ar/index.htm (August 27, 2018).

CHAPTER 5: CHANGING SOCIETY: GENDER AND RACE

1. Zim, "All-American Girls Professional Baseball League," History by Zim: Beyond the Textbooks, June 19, 2013, www.historybyzim.com/2013/06/all-american-girls -professional-baseball-league (July 5, 2018).

2. "Statue Facts," The Statue of Liberty—Ellis Island Foundation, www.libertyellis foundation.org/statue-facts (July 5, 2018).

3. Jeremy Fuchs, "NHL's First Female Goalie Continues to Inspire," *Sports Illustrated*, June 27, 2016, www.si.com/nhl/2016/06/27/manon-rheaume-where-are-they -now (August 9, 2018).

4. Lizzy Acker, "Portland Nicknames Explained," *Oregonian/*OregonLive, June 2016, www.oregonlive.com/portland/index.ssf/2016/06/portlands_nicknames_explained .html (September 5, 2018).

5. Max Kutner, "Real-Life Women Last Appeared on US Paper Money 100 Years Ago; Black People Never Have," *Newsweek*, April 20, 2016, www.newsweek.com/ history-women-currency-tubman-anderson-450414 (September 5, 2018).

6. Michael Gliozzi, "The History of Baseball in Pittsburgh," Popular Pittsburgh, November 24, 2014, http://popularpittsburgh.com/baseballhistory (July 15, 2018).

7. "Toni Stone," Biography.com, www.biography.com/people/toni-stone-40319 (August 5, 2018).

8. "Cuban Giants," Negro League Baseball Players' Association, www.nlbpa.com/the-negro-league-teams/cuban-giants (August 5, 2018).

9. Karen Guenther, "SPHAs," Encyclopedia of Greater Philadelphia, https://philadelphiaencyclopedia.org/archive/sphas (January 10, 2018).

CHAPTER 6: THE NATURAL WORLD

1. Richard Bak, *A Narrative History of Tiger Stadium* (Detroit: Wayne State University Press, 1998), 58–59.

2. "Cincinnati Bengals," Team Name Origin, http://teamnameorigin.com/nfl/nickname/cincinnati-bengals (September 11, 2018).

3. "The Tigers," Tigers in Crisis, www.tigersincrisis.com/the_tigers.htm (September 10, 2018).

4. Thales Exoo, "Ask Chicagoist: Why Are They Called the Bears?" *Chicagoist*, January 31, 2017, https://web.archive.org/web/20170510153921/http://chicagoist.com/2007/01/31/ask_chicagoist_why_are_they_called_the_bears.php (September 10, 2018).

5. "Grizzly Bear," Speed of Animals, www.speedofanimals.com/animals/grizzly_bear (August 5, 2018).

6. Matt Blitz, "Why the Chicago Cubs Are Named after a Baby Bear," Today I Found Out, July 26, 2017, www.todayifoundout.com/index.php/2017/07/chicago-cubs-named-baby-bear-long-weird-history-mascot (September 5, 2018).

7. "Behind the Name: Grizzlies," NBA.com, May 12, 2006, www.nba.com/grizzlies/features/feature-060512-behind_the_name.html (January 5, 2018).

8. "Gray Wolf," Minnesota Department of Natural Resources, www.dnr.state.mn.us/mammals/wolves/mgmt.html (September 26, 2018).

9. "Michigan," 50States.com, www.50states.com/bio/nickname3.htm (September 3, 2018).

10. "Wisconsin," Netstate.com, www.netstate.com/states/intro/wi_intro.htm (July 10, 2018).

11. James Dator, "What Animal Inspired the Nashville Predators Logo?" *SBNation*, May 23, 2017, www.sbnation.com/lookit/2017/5/23/15680256/nashville-predators-logo-badass-cat-skull-discovered-in-ancient-cave-nhl-stanley-cup (September 5, 2018).

12. "CU Logo Evolution Fact Sheet," Colorado Buffaloes, https://cubuffs.com/sports/2005/5/10/119691.aspx (September 9, 2018).

13. "Scot Who Saved American Buffalo," Electric Scotland, www.electricscotland.com/history/articles/buffalo.htm (August 1, 2018).

14. "Buffalo Bills," Primarily A Capella, www.singers.com/group/Buffalo-Bills (July 1, 2018).

15. "William F. 'Buffalo Bill' Cody," Buffalo Bill Center of the West, https://centerofthewest.org/explore/buffalo-bill/research/buffalo-bill (August 10, 2018).

16. "Animal Fact Sheet: Western Diamondback Rattlesnake," Arizona-Sonora Desert Museum, www.desertmuseum.org/kids/oz/long-fact-sheets/Diamondback%20Rattlesnake.php (September 1, 2018).

17. "What Is CTE?" Concussion Legacy Foundation, https://concussionfoundation.org/CTE-resources/what-is-CTE (September 1, 2018).

18. Scott Allen, "How All 32 NFL Teams Got Their Names," *Mental Floss*, September 9, 2018, http://mentalfloss.com/article/25650/whats-nickname-origins-all-32-nfl-team-names (September 9, 2018).

19. "Panther," A–Z Animals, https://a-z-animals.com/animals/panther (September 1, 2018).

20. "Fun Jaguar Facts for Kids," Science Kids, www.sciencekids.co.nz/sciencefacts/animals/jaguar.html (August 5, 2018).

21. "Siberian Huskies," VetStreet, www.vetstreet.com/dogs/siberian-husky (September 4, 2018).

22. Josie Turner, "The True Story of Balto, the Dog That Became a Hero," AnimalWised, April 23, 2017, www.animalwised.com/the-true-story-of-balto-the-dog-that-became-a-hero-1394.html (August 1, 2018).

23. "Handsome Dan," The Official Website of Yale University Athletics, www.yalebulldogs.com/information/mascot/handsome_dan/index (June 5, 2018).

24. "Damn Good Dogs," Terry College of Business Lecture Series, http://www.youtube.com/watch?v=HlnmhIP9v8U (February 23, 2019).

25. "Stingers Pay Ga. Tech $600,000 in Buzz Suit," *Deseret News*, October 2, 2001, www.deseretnews.com/article/866938/Stingers-pay-Ga-Tech-600000-in-Buzz-suit.html (July 5, 2018).

CHAPTER 7: GEOGRAPHY

1. "The Volunteer State," State Symbols USA, https://statesymbolsusa.org/symbol-official-item/tennessee/state-nickname/volunteer-state (July 5, 2018).

2. "Remember the Alamo," Encyclopedia.com, www.encyclopedia.com/history/dictionaries-thesauruses-pictures-and-press-releases/remember-alamo (June 7, 2018).

3. "What Is a Vandal?" University of Idaho Vandals, https://govandals.com/sports/2016/7/13/what-is-a-vandal.aspx (August 7, 2018).

4. NU Athletic Communications, "Origin of the Cornhusker Name," Nebraska Athletics, July 24, 2017, www.huskers.com/ViewArticle.dbml?DB_OEM_ID=100&ATCLID=2802 (July 17, 2018).

5. "San Diego de Alcala," California Mission Background and History, www.californiamissionguide.com/mission-guide/san-diego-de-alcala (July 7, 2018).

6. "Pelicans," *National Geographic*, www.nationalgeographic.com/animals/birds/group/pelicans (August 7, 2018).

7. Armand J. Eardley and Richard A. Marston, "Rocky Mountains," *Encyclopedia Britannica*, https://web.archive.org/web/20170812144910/https://www.britannica.com/place/Rocky-Mountains (August 9, 2018).

8. "What Is an Avalanche?" Conserve Energy Future, www.conserve-energy-future.com/types-causes-effects-of-avalanches.php (July 7, 2018).

9. Chet Orloff, "Portland Penny," Oregon Encyclopedia, last updated March 17, 2018, https://oregonencyclopedia.org/articles/portland_penny/#.W7Zq6LQm5ok (September 28, 2018).

10. "Did You Know? 10 Facts about the San Andreas Fault," Geology In, February 2016, www.geologyin.com/2016/02/did-you-know-10-facts-about-san-andreas.html (September 1, 2018).

11. Andy Kelly, "Royal Arsenal FC Turn Professional—The Truth," *Arsenal History* (blog), May 9, 2017, www.thearsenalhistory.com/?cat=38 (August 5, 2018).

12. "Pittsburgh Penguins," Team Name Origin, http://teamnameorigin.com/nhl/nickname/pittsburgh-penguins (August 5, 2018).

13. Wilma Dykeman, "Appalachian Mountains," *Encyclopedia Britannica*, www.britannica.com/place/Appalachian-Mountains (August 5, 2018).

14. "Team History: Falcons," Pro Football Hall of Fame, www.profootballhof.com/teams/atlanta-falcons/team-history (June 7, 2018).

15. Dave McCracken, "Gold Panning Instructions," The New 49ers, www.goldgold.com/gold-prospectinggold-panning-instructions.html (August 19, 2018).

CHAPTER 8: INDUSTRIAL REVOLUTION

1. "Uses of Steel Materials in America," Mid City Steel, http://midcitysteel.com/uses-of-steel-materials-in-america-a-history (August 7, 2018).

2. "Logos and Uniforms of the Pittsburgh Steelers," Wikipedia, https://en.wikipedia.org/wiki/Logos_and_uniforms_of_the_Pittsburgh_Steelers (July 5, 2018).

3. Cathal Brennan, "The Molly Maguires," Irish Story, July 9, 2013, www.theirishstory.com/2013/07/09/the-molly-maguires/#.W7aO6LQm5ok (July 5, 2018).

4. "Green Bay Packers," Team Name Origin, http://teamnameorigin.com/nfl/nickname/green-bay-packers (August 10, 2018).

5. "Naming a Team: The Story Behind the Blue Jackets Name," NHL.com, November 11, 2005, www.nhl.com/bluejackets/news/naming-a-team-the-story-behind-the-blue-jackets-name/c-479316 (June 6, 2018).

6. "Behind the Name—Detroit Pistons," NBA.com, August 16, 2006, www.nba.com/pistons/features/behindthename.html (May 5, 2017).

7. "Rockets in Ancient Times (100 B.C. to 17th Century)," MSFC History Office, https://history.msfc.nasa.gov/rocketry/tl1.html (May 5, 2018).

8. "Traditions: The Racers," Murray State Racers, https://goracers.com/sports/2005/10/31/730171800.aspx (September 6, 2018).

9. "Clipper Ship," *Encyclopedia Britannica*, www.britannica.com/technology/clipper-ship (September 19, 2018).

CHAPTER 9: FOREIGN STUDIES

1. "Ancient Egyptian Sports: Hockey," Tour Egypt, www.touregypt.net/historical essays/ancsportsa1.htm (July 7, 2018).

2. Jamie Fitzpatrick, "Why the Montreal Canadiens Are Called the Habs," Thought co. 2019, https://www.thoughtco.com/montreal-canadiens-called-the-habs-2778720 (February 23, 2019).

3. "Toronto Maple Leafs," Team Names, www.teamnames.net/worldwide/ice -hockey/toronto-maple-leafs (August 30, 2018).

4. "Edmonton," Canadian Encyclopedia 2017, https://www.thecanadian encyclopedia.ca/en/article/edmonton (February 23, 2019).

5. "Dinosaur Provincial Park," *Encyclopedia Britannica*, www.britannica.com/place/Dinosaur-Provincial-Park (June 7, 2018).

6. "Canucks History," Vancouver Canucks, http://canucks.ice.nhl.com/club/page .htm?id=40019 (June 30, 2018).

7. Ellie Griffiths, "The History of Waltzing Matilda," Culture Trip, August 12, 2016, https://theculturetrip.com/pacific/australia/articles/the-history-of-waltzing -matilda (September 30, 2018).

8. "Great Australian Bight," Australia: The Land Where Time Began, last updated October 21, 2016, https://austhrutime.com/great_australian_bight_marine_park.htm (September 25, 2018).

9. "Why Is Japan Called the Land of the Rising Sun?" Reference.com, www.reference .com/geography/japan-called-land-rising-sun-d0c4a5f1f7f3fbb1 (June 5, 2018).

10. "Wichita History, Facts and Timeline," World Guides.com, www.world-guides .com/north-america/usa/kansas/wichita/wichita_history.html (June 5, 2017).

CHAPTER 10: PEOPLE AND POLITICS

1. "What Is a Hoosier?" Indiana Historical Bureau, www.in.gov/history/2612.htm (July 5, 2018).

2. "Cavalier," *Oxford English Dictionary*, https://en.oxforddictionaries.com/definition/cavalier (July 5, 2018).

3. "A Piece of American Royal History," American Royal, www.americanroyal.com/about/our-history (September 1, 2018).

4. "Abraham Lincoln Quotes," BrainyQuote, www.brainyquote.com/quotes/abraham_lincoln_109275 (August 9, 2018).

5. Jane Bennett Clark, "Watersmeet Nimrods: Life after the Spotlight," *Kiplinger's Personal Finance*, March 2016, www.kiplinger.com/article/business/T049-C000-S002 -watersmeet-nimrods-life-after-the-spotlight.html (May 10, 2017).

6. "Ohio's State Nickname," Ohio History Central, www.ohiohistorycentral .org/w/Ohio%27s_State_Nickname (May 5, 2018).

7. Donald W. Worcester, "Longhorn Cattle," Texas State Historical Association, last updated May 23, 2017, https://tshaonline.org/handbook/online/articles/atl02 (May 5, 2018).

8. "A History of Spurs," Sporting Collection, www.sportingcollection.com/spurs/history-spurs.html (May 4, 2018).

9. "Dallas Chaparrals Team History," Sports Team History, https://sportsteam history.com/dallas-chaparrals (September 1, 2018).

10. "History of West Point," Army West Point https://goarmywestpoint.com/sports/2015/3/6/GEN_2014010169.aspx (September 10, 2018).

11. Juliet Macur, "A Sport Banned by Mao Zedong Makes a Comeback," *New York Times*, July 6, 2008, www.nytimes.com/2008/07/06/sports/06iht-base.1.14264507 .html (July 1, 2018).

CHAPTER 11: MARINE SCIENCES AND METEOROLOGY

1. "Ponce de Leon," History Channel, last updated August 21, 2018, www.history .com/topics/exploration/juan-ponce-de-leon (September 5, 2108).

2. "Dolphin," Online Etymology Dictionary, www.etymonline.com/word/Dolphin (September 1, 2018).

3. "Marlin," *Encyclopedia Britannica* 2018, www.britannica.com/animal/marlin (September 5, 2018).

4. Amanda Green, "16 Fun Facts about Tortoises," *Mental Floss*, May 23, 2014, http://mentalfloss.com/article/56805/16-fun-facts-about-tortoises (August 30, 2018).

5. Gregory McNamee, "Seattle," *Encyclopedia Britannica*, last updated January 27, 2017, www.britannica.com/place/Seattle-Washington (September 5, 2018).

6. "What Kind of Bird Is a Seahawk?" 10,000 Birds, January 19, 2006, www.10000birds.com/seahawk.htm (May 5, 2018).

7. "Fun Facts: Phoenix, Arizona," VisitPhoenix, www.visitphoenix.com/media/media-kit/fun-facts (July 7, 2018).

8. Mark Cartwright, "Olmec Civilization," Ancient History Encyclopedia, April 4, 2018, www.ancient.eu/Olmec_Civilization (June 7, 2018).

9. "Earth Science for Kids: Weather–Hurricanes (Tropical Cyclones)," Ducksters Education Site, www.ducksters.com/science/earth_science/hurricanes.php (August 4, 2018).

CHAPTER 12: ELECTIVES AND INDEPENDENT STUDIES

1. "1845 Original Rules of Baseball," OpenSite, http://open-site.org/Sports/Baseball/History/Rules/1845_Original_Rules_of_Baseball (July 7, 2018).

2. John DeGange, "Ins and Outs," *New London (CT) Evening Day*, April 16, 1953, https://news.google.com/newspapers?id=F-wgAAAAIBAJ&sjid=LHIFAAAAIBAJ&pg=1920,2741323&dq=red+legs+name+change (July 10, 2018).

3. "Boston Red Sox History," Fenway Ticket King, www.fenwayticketking.com/redsoxhistory.html (July 7, 2018).

4. "History of Alabama Football," RollTideBama.com, https://web.archive.org/web/20081205041602/http://rolltidebama.com/history.htm (August 4, 2018).

5. Mark Nothaft, "Is Scottsdale Community College's Mascot Really an Artichoke?" *Arizona Republic*, October 4, 2016, www.azcentral.com/story/news/local/scottsdale-contributor/2016/10/04/scottsdale-community-colleges-mascot-really-artichoke/91149908 (July 5, 2017).

6. "Rubber Duck," National Toy Hall of Fame, www.toyhalloffame.org/toys/rubber-duck (August 7, 2018).

7. Hannah Keyser, "Why Is Connecticut Called the Nutmeg State?" *Mental Floss*, March 5, 2014 http://mentalfloss.com/article/55245/why-connecticut-called-nutmeg-state (June 7, 2018).

8. "Connecticut History," ConneCT Kids, www.ct.gov/kids/cwp/view.asp?q=329084 (September 5, 2018).

SUGGESTED READINGS

Here are some suggested readings that have made an impact on me over the years. They are all relevant to the subject matter presented in this book. The list includes five of my young adult novels inspired by team sports.

Angell, Roger. *The Summer Game.* Lincoln: University of Nebraska Press–Bison Books, 2004.
Angell is a poetic writer who masterfully illuminates baseball's position in the world.

Bouton, Jim. *Ball Four: My Life and Hard Times Throwing the Knuckleball in the Big Leagues.* New York: World, 1970.
A season-long diary by a pitcher for the expansion 1969 Seattle Pilots. It broke all the rules of social secrecy in baseball. (Contains some mature content.)

Brasher, William. *The Bingo Long Traveling All-Stars and Motor Kings.* Champaign: University of Illinois Press, 1993.
A look at life in the Negro Leagues during the Jim Crow era.

Dryden, Ken. *The Game.* Hoboken, NJ: Wiley, 1993.
A critically acclaimed work by a former NHL goalie who won six Stanley Cups with the Montreal Canadiens.

Plimpton, George. *Paper Lion.* New York: Harper & Row, 1966.
A real-life Walter Mitty–like tale of a journalist attempting to play quarterback with the NFL's Detroit Lions during the preseason.

Pluto, Terry. *Loose Balls: The Short, Wild Life of the American Basketball Association.* New York: Simon & Schuster, 1990.
A fun and insightful look into a financially troubled sports league attempting to survive. (Contains some mature content.)

Tackach, James, and Joshua Stein. *Fields of Summer: America's Great Ballparks.* New York: Moore & Moore, 1992.
A virtual walking tour of the United States' most amazing ballparks, past and present.

Treat, Roger. *The Encyclopedia of Football.* New York: Barnes, 1974.
Famed journalist and historian Roger Treat provides the reader a substantial immersion into the history and relevance of football.

Volponi, Paul. *Black and White.* New York: Viking, 2006.
Two high school basketball stars and best friends, one black and one white, experience the criminal justice system differently after committing a crime together. (Contains coarse language.)

——. *Hurricane Song.* New York: Viking, 2008.
A high school football player reconnects with his dad while riding out Hurricane Katrina in the Superdome, the home of the New Orleans Saints. (Contains coarse language.)

——. *The Final Four.* New York: Viking, 2012.
A quartet of college basketball players from different backgrounds compete for the Michigan State Spartans and the Trojans of Troy as they meet in a semifinal game of the NCAA Basketball Tournament.

——. *Game Seven.* New York: Viking, 2015.
A teen Cuban refugee escapes to the United States where his father, an ace relief pitcher for the Marlins, is competing in the World Series against the Yankees.

——. *Top Prospect.* Minneapolis, MN: Lerner, 2015
An eighth-grader receives an early college football scholarship to play for the Gators, his hometown team. (Middle grade)

INDEX

ABOUT THE AUTHOR

Paul Volponi is a writer, educator, and journalist living in New York City. He is the award-winning author of twelve novels for young adults, and the recipient of twelve American Library Association honors. *Black and White* is the winner of the International Reading Association's Children's Book Award. That novel of social justice was inspired by the six years the author worked on Rikers Island (the world's biggest jail) teaching incarcerated teens to read and write. *The Final Four*, about the men's NCAA Basketball Tournament, received five starred reviews and is on the NYC Chancellor's Ninth-Grade Reading List (NYC Reads 365). *Top Prospect*, a middle-grade novel about an eighth-grader given an early college football scholarship, is part of Scholastic's nationwide book club.

The author holds an MA in American literature from the City College of New York and a BA in English from Baruch College.

You can read excerpts from all of Paul Volponi's YA novels, discover their origins, and read the author's notes at http://paulvolponibooks.com, or visit him on Facebook.